Rudolf Steiner
and
Christian Rosenkreutz

It has only now become possible again to find the wellspring of
Rosicrucian wisdom and let it flow into the general culture ...

Christian Rosenkreutz has always lived among us and
he is with us now as our guide in spiritual life.

Rudolf Steiner[1]

RUDOLF STEINER
AND
CHRISTIAN ROSENKREUTZ

with a translation of the
Fama Fraternitatis
by Thomas Vaughan (1652)

PETER SELG

2012
STEINERBOOKS

SteinerBooks
610 Main Street, Great Barrington, MA 01230
www.steinerbooks.org

Translated by Margot M. Saar

Originally published in German as *Rudolf Steiner und Christian
Rosenkreutz* by Verlag des Ita Wegman Instituts, Arlesheim,
Switzerland 2010.

Library of Congress Cataloging-in-Publication Data

Selg, Peter, 1963-
[Rudolf Steiner und Christian Rosenkreutz. English]
Rudolf Steiner and Christian Rosenkreutz : with the Fama fraternitatis
translated by Thomas Vaughan (1652) / Peter Selg ; [translated by
Margot M. Saar].
  p. cm.
Includes bibliographical references (p.   ).
ISBN 978-0-88010-660-3
  1. Steiner, Rudolf, 1861-1925. 2. Rosencreutz, Christian. 3.
Rosicrucians. I. Fama fraternitatis. English. II. Title.
  BP595.S895S379513 2012
  299'.935--dc23
                                                    2012012444

Contents

For Traute Page-Lafrenz

10/22/12

Introduction

Only the initiates know who Christian Rosenkreutz is
and what stands behind him.[2]   —RUDOLF STEINER

Rudolf Steiner spoke in many lectures about the relationship
between anthroposophical spiritual science and Rosicrucianism.[3]
References to the "essence of Christian Rosenkreutz"[4] are found
much more rarely; and for a very good reason: "One needs
immense faith in the mysteries of spiritual life to speak about
Christian Rosenkreutz—faith not in the person, but in the great
secrets of spiritual life" (Neuchâtel, September 27, 1911).[5] While
Steiner certainly had that faith, he could not expect to find it to the
same degree in his audience, and was therefore reluctant to refer to
Christian Rosenkreutz in public lectures.[6] Paul Regenstreif wrote:
"Rudolf Steiner often made reference to Christian Rosenkreutz's
mission and tasks, but never described him in any detail."[7]

According to Rudolf Steiner, Christian Rosenkreutz was one
of the "great leaders of humanity,"[8] whose task it was to lead the
esoteric movement into modern times,[9] or, to "lead the esoteric
movement into the future."[10] He was the "great servant of Christ
Jesus"[11] and the "greatest teacher of Christianity,"[12] who carried
on the impulse "imparted by Christ Jesus when he came to earth
to undergo the Mystery of Golgotha."[13] In his anthroposophical lectures, Rudolf Steiner often pointed out that humanity
depended for its further evolution on a growing understanding
of the deeds of Christ, on the true knowledge of Christianity and
of the Christ. To "lead the esoteric movement into the future"
means to prepare and teach Christian knowledge and to support
any effort that aims at enabling Christ's original intentions and
impulse stream into civilization: "The spiritual stream related to

Christian Rosenkreutz offers the most potent assistance to those
who strive *to understand the Christ impulse.*"[14]

*

For Rudolf Steiner, Christian Rosenkreutz was not the
unknown, mythical founder of an esoteric community but a
specific, "unique" individuality.[15] In 1912 in Hamburg he referred
to Rosenkreutz, surprisingly, as a "noble martyr," "who endured
through his way of working, and, more than any other person, will
endure in the future. I say 'person', for the suffering of Christ was
the suffering of a god. This has to do with the great dangers that
the truth will have to face in the future."[16] Christian Rosenkreutz's
suffering—during and in between his various incarnations—is
not over. According to Rudolf Steiner, his suffering is connected
with humanity having fallen behind in its spiritual responsibili-
ties, tasks, and duties; in its self-knowledge and its knowledge
of the world. "The light shines in the darkness but the darkness
comprehended it not," John the evangelist (Lazarus-John) wrote
soon after the Mystery of Golgotha.[17] Speaking about Christian
Rosenkreutz in Berlin on June 20, 1912, Rudolf Steiner said:

> [...] The martyrdom of Christian Rosenkreutz will be
> caused by the fact that most people are reluctant to look
> into their own souls in search of the evolving individuality
> or to face the inconvenience that the truth is not served on
> a platter but has to be found through intense inner effort
> and struggle. There can be no other way in the name of the
> individuality that is known as Christian Rosenkreutz.[18]

Spiritual truth will have to undergo "great dangers" in the
future, according to Rudolf Steiner. It needs to be achieved through
self-knowledge and profound threshold experiences, while any
kind of "personality cult,"[19] with its attending Luciferic tempta-
tions, needs to be resolutely rejected. "These Luciferic influences
are very strong and will grow even stronger."[20]

Rudolf Steiner's indications are likely to refer to spirituality as it presents itself today and in the future. Occult knowledge that was kept concealed for so long is now freely available. Spiritually gifted people of all descriptions appear in public, taking in the masses with their esoteric glamour and sensationalism. Rudolf Steiner chose the way of Christian Rosenkreutz, whose task it was to prepare the dissemination of spiritual knowledge while he himself remained in the background. His path is that of individual self-knowledge, of developing inner judgment through the study of spiritual content ("the less people **believe** in authority, the more will they understand Christian Rosenkreutz"[21]). Rudolf Steiner practiced and taught that approach throughout his life, and as we can see from his biography, he built his entire work on it. He hoped that his pupils would also find the right access to modern spiritual science. "Only those who examine carefully what comes out of the spiritual worlds will remain faithful to Christian Rosenkreutz."[22]

The present study is a small contribution to Rudolf Steiner's 150th birthday (February 27, 2011). *Some aspects* of Steiner's descriptions of Christian Rosenkreutz are considered, while others are left out, such as the sequence of incarnations that has been studied and written about by Hella Krause-Zimmer and Hella Wiesberger.[23] The wide panorama Rudolf Steiner opened up with his references to the stream of Christian Rosenkreutz holds some central aspects that must not be overlooked. They will form the center of the following study. Since those aspects also bear on Rudolf Steiner and on our approach to him and his work in our times, it seems necessary and justified to call attention to them. No claim shall be made in this study of having fully grasped and presented the spiritual relationship between Rudolf Steiner and Christian Rosenkreutz in all its profundity and complexity. It is a relationship that belongs to the "great mysteries of spiritual life" and to the sphere of knowledge reserved to initiates.[24]

PETER SELG
September 2010, Yonges Island, USA

1.

"The great servant of Christ Jesus"

Rudolf Steiner's Portrayal of Christian Rosenkreutz

Rudolf Steiner's rose cross (reverse)

FRIEDRICH RITTELMEYER published the following passage in 1928 in his memoirs of Rudolf Steiner. It was the fruit of several hours of confidential biographical conversations that he had had with his teacher many years earlier (late July/early August 1915). He wrote:

Rudolf Steiner's descriptions of the great teachers who crossed his path were most impressive. Extraordinary, spiritual people, wholly unknown to the public, appeared at the right hour. They helped him to discover and develop his faculties in the decisive years; and they stood witness, as it were, when the mission of his life lit up. Even without Rudolf Steiner's words, it was clear to us that such a life is prepared long in advance, that the necessary helpers are sent at the right moment, and that all things come together in one event that intervenes full of wisdom and insight in the history of humanity. The external world knows nothing of this. The life of a leader of humanity, who has a mission at the highest level, is a work of art on which angels and human beings work together. It was amazing to hear directly and in such detail that spiritual leaders of humanity really exist who, although concealed, guide the history of humanity actively and presciently. Just think how the unknown intervened in the life of Jacob Boehme, how the Friend of God appeared in the life of John Tauler, and you will understand what Rudolf Steiner meant at the time. The difference is that the sublime leaders were perceived more consciously and clearly then in their guidance toward an important task on earth. However alien that world seemed compared to the everyday world, we felt at home there when we listened to Rudolf Steiner's account of it. I will never forget the look in Rudolf Steiner's eyes when he said of one of these two spiritual individuals, "He was a very important individuality!" One had the impression his gaze followed that individuality for a long time. In his gaze was the kind of reverence that one great sage feels for another. He told me later that he had once been rescued by a "Master" when he was about to do something that would have led to his certain death. When I asked him whether one of the two was still alive and whether he saw him occasionally, he replied, "I have no need for that." He felt secure because he was able to establish a spiritual connection at any time, without any physical presence.[25]

Rittelmeyer had heard more about Steiner's "masters" from him than he was willing to disclose in his publication. He did, however, intimate this to some of his friends. After a conversation with Rittelmeyer on July 9, 1924, Walter Johannes Stein wrote in his diary: "Rittelm[eyer] says, when he was asked to write a short biography of Rudolf Steiner, Steiner told him in the presence of Mrs. Steiner that he had two initiators: Christian Rosenkreutz and Master Jesus (Zarathustra). *The latter referred him to Fichte. The former worked through Felix Balde*" [author's emphasis].[26] Elsewhere Steiner also spoke of the occult master who had conducted his esoteric training (most probably in 1880[27]) supported by the works of Fichte.[28] Stein and Rittelmeyer, also Edouard Schuré, seemed to indicate that this was Master Jesus (Zarathustra):[29] the individuality who prepared Christ's incarnation in the body of Jesus of Nazareth at the turning point of time; an individuality who has remained active ever since.[30] He approached Rudolf Steiner in the shape of an ordinary man, whose identity could not be established. Steiner told Rittelmeyer that Christian Rosenkreutz had worked on him *through* "Felix Balde," that is, through the simple herb gatherer Felix Koguzki (1831–1909) from Trumau. Rudolf Steiner had met Koguzki in the fall of 1879 and was referred by him to the second (or actual) master.[31] In his autobiography, Rudolf Steiner wrote about Felix

Koguzki, who appears as the character Felix Balde in the mystery dramas: "As a personality he seemed to be the organ of a spiritual content that wanted to speak out of occult worlds."[32] "I am but the instrument of powers that grant me speech," Felix says in the mystery drama.[33]

After Rudolf Steiner had entered the technical college both masters approached him through unimposing personalities, a fact that made a deep impression on Friedrich Rittelmeyer. Rudolf Steiner spoke about this aspect of esoteric leaders today in a general lecture:

> Today's leaders walk around on earth in human shape unrecognized by the exoteric world. If we would speak in spiritual science of the masters of wisdom and of the harmony of feelings,[34] people would wonder at the simplicity and unostentatious humanity of these masters in all countries. They exist on the physical plane, yet their most important lessons are not taught on the physical, but on the spiritual plane. Those who want to hear them and receive their teachings, need to find access not only to their physical, incarnated body, but to their spiritual essence.[35]

Among the "teachings" received by Rudolf Steiner through Felix Koguzki (or the spiritual individuality behind Koguzki) was the mystery knowledge of nature beings and the healing power of plants. Felix was "fully initiated into the secrets of all plants, how they work and how they relate to the cosmos and to human nature," Rudolf Steiner would write four-times-seven years later.[36] Through Felix's special and unusual individuality Rudolf Steiner came to meet "ancient" wisdom, ancient esoteric nature wisdom.[37] Christian Rosenkreutz was actively at work in the *transition* from the old to the new wisdom, which was to come with Rudolf Steiner's anthroposophic spiritual science. He clearly prepared and shaped that transition, as the one who would "lead the esoteric movement into the future."

Felix Koguzki. Trumau, 1906

From Friedrich Rittelmeyer we also know that Rudolf Steiner had once been saved by one of the two "masters." In 1911, on the day before Michaelmas, Rudolf Steiner explained in a lecture he gave in Neuchâtel that before 1899 (before the end of the "Kali Yuga"), Christian Rosenkreutz had often used a "karmic crisis," usually a life-saving act, to call those who belonged to him to work with him. They would place their newly given lives in the service of spiritual Rosicrucianism, or of the human development that Rosenkreutz helped to make possible. (Since then, the "calling" has come to be an inner experience of soul and spirit.) According to Rudolf Steiner, such a biographical intervention was the result of an encounter with Christian Rosenkreutz before birth. The memory of that encounter made itself felt in the conscious (or close-to-conscious) reception of a will impulse after the life-saving event had taken place. Steiner described scenes (various forms) of a calling through Christian Rosenkreutz in numerous lectures. His description of February 9, 1912, in Vienna probably contained autobiographical elements to which he would refer in his conversations with Rittelmeyer many years later. ("He told me later that he had once been rescued by a 'Master' when he was about to do something that would have led to his certain death.") In Vienna Rudolf Steiner said, after describing a life-saving intervention by Christian Rosenkreutz:

> I have particularly emphasized this most eminent experience of a calling. I could use other events that relate directly to the spiritual world that can be found in the life between death and birth, *but in our spiritual context it is precisely this event that should seem significant to us, because it has to do with our spiritual movement.*[38] [author's emphasis added].

Rudolf Steiner gave the following account as an example of a calling by Christian Rosenkreutz:

Imagine a person lying in bed. (I have used other examples in other places, and they are all accurate.) Suddenly he wakes up without knowing why. As if by instinct, his gaze is drawn to a wall that is usually dark. The room is faintly lit; the wall is dark. Suddenly, writing appears on the wall: "Rise instantly!" Although it seems strange to him, he gets up. He leaves the house. He has hardly stepped out of the house when the ceiling above his bed collapses. (Nobody else was in any danger.) It would certainly have killed him. He makes inquiries everywhere; there is no one on the physical plane who had warned him to get up. If he had stayed in bed he would have died.[39]

It is not certain whether the incident described by Steiner in Vienna was autobiographical. He spoke of it as an intervention in someone's life by Christian Rosenkreutz that went beyond an encounter with the individuality through whom Rosenkreutz was active. The earthly representatives of Christian Rosenkreutz and Master Jesus who crossed his path in and around Vienna were important to him, and Rudolf Steiner held them in high esteem throughout his life. They, on their part, established the connection to the spiritual masters who stood behind them and whose "messengers" they were. ("On the physical plane they [the masters] work through the 'messengers' sent by them."[40]) Rudolf Steiner remained in connection with the masters throughout his life.

*

Toward the end of his life Rudolf Steiner wrote in the *Leading Thoughts* that the Rosicrucians longed for a true meeting with the archangel Michael. The Rosicrucians, who prepared the earth for Michael's influence, had not been able to see the cosmic "countenance of the Christ" on earth prior to 1879.[41] With Rosenkreutz (and Master Jesus) as his inner companions, Rudolf

Steiner began his science studies in Vienna after 1879/80. His studies were associated with the need to overcome the scientific materialism that constituted a, if not *the*, Michaelic challenge of the present and future. Later, his scientific studies led him to Goethe, who had a deep connection with Rosicrucianism,[42] and who had inspired and initiated the spiritualization of the natural sciences at the dawn of the nineteenth century. Steiner's further journey led him, in the company of the masters, to a deep encounter with the Christ mystery.

Some time later Rudolf Steiner referred to Master Jesus as the one who had inspired the Christian esoteric schools (of Paul and Dionysius the Areopagite), describing him as "the greatest helper of those who strove to understand the important event of Palestine."[43] "He [Master Jesus] stands behind the great spiritual figures of Christianity, forever teaching the true meaning of the important event of Palestine."[44] Master Jesus also worked through the "Friend of God from the Oberland" on German mysticism, a stream that through its highest representatives infused a spiritual concept of the Christ into the prevailing culture. Among these representatives were the Dominican philosophers John Tauler and Meister Eckhart; and later, the German idealist thinkers Schelling, Hegel, and Fichte.[45] Rudolf Steiner's "standing before the Mystery of Golgotha" was intimately related to the activity of Master Jesus, as was his first theosophical publication *Mystics after Modernism*.

> The Christianity I sought was not to be found in any of the creeds…. I had to enter deeply into Christianity, and found myself in the world where the spirit itself speaks of it.
>
> …
>
> Having stood spiritually before the Mystery of Golgotha in a deep and solemn celebration of knowledge was highly important for the development of my soul.[46]

Theosophie

Einführung in übersinnliche
Welterkenntnis und Menschenbestimmung

von

Dr. Rudolf Steiner

BERLIN
C. A. Schwetschke und Sohn
1904

Original edition of Rudolf Steiner's *Theosophy*, Berlin, 1904

It was on the basis of his publication *Mystics after Modernism* and the subsequent *Christianity as Mystical Fact,* which was intimately connected with Christian Rosenkreutz, that Rudolf Steiner was offered a position of responsibility in the Theosophical Society soon after the turn of the twentieth century. Leading English theosophists referred to his writings as *"the true Theosophy"* because they felt that they reflected the Theosophical Society's original intentions.[47] [author's emphasis].

Rudolf Steiner knew that his early books on the theory and method of knowledge, and his introductions to Goethe's natural-scientific writings, complied with the intentions of Christian Rosenkreutz and Master Jesus. "Those who read these introductions will find in them theosophical ideas veiled as philosophical idealism. ...The occult powers that stand behind me advised me to present 'everything as idealist philosophy.'"[48] Steiner's attitude to the members and followers of the Theosophical Society remained ambivalent. There was spiritual attraction, but he kept a certain distance. Despite outer tensions, he recognized after 1900 that the spiritual powers he wanted and had to serve were associated with the Theosophical Society, and so he decided to become active in that society. Later he said that the Theosophical Society, which had been founded in New York in 1875, had Rosicrucian roots.[49] In 1905, he wrote in a letter to his first collaborator, Marie von Sivers, that he had served the Theosophical Society not just in agreement with the powers that guided him, but on their request.

> Not a day passes without the resounding admonition from the Masters: "Be cautious, consider the immaturity of your time. You are dealing with children, and it is your destiny that you have to bring the highest esoteric teachings to mere children. Be aware that through your words you educate villains." I can assure you that if the Master had not known how to persuade me, I would have continued to write philosophical books and speak about literature and

philosophy *after* 1901, despite the need for theosophy in our age.[50]

In a lecture Rudolf Steiner said that although the masters conveyed impulses, they did not take decisions and actions away from those associated with them. *"They [people] receive impulses, but they have to put them into practice out of their own spirituality."*[51] This applied to Rudolf Steiner's first books on the theory of knowledge and Goetheanism, which complied with the intention of the masters. It applied equally to his decision to take on a responsible position within the Theosophical Society.

Rudolf Steiner spoke about the leading esoteric masters in October 1903 at the first General Meeting of the German Section of the Theosophical Society. The first part of his "occult historical research...the future teaching program" (Wiesberger) was to consist of the "teachings of the great spiritual leaders of humanity.... Occult historical research will teach us how leaders of humanity can rise to heights where they can take on divine missions."[52] It is not known how successful Rudolf Steiner was in conveying this to his theosophical audience in the fall of 1903. Soon after, when his book *Theosophy* was published (in May 1904), he began to speak about Christian Rosenkreutz in public lectures as well. At the same time, he started an esoteric school in which Christian Rosenkreutz and Master Jesus played an important part.

*

On May 30, 1904, in a public lecture about the rise of Central European occult societies in connection with mystery knowledge and mysticism, delivered at the Architect's House in Berlin, Rudolf Steiner said:

We observe how at the time of the middle of the Middle Ages secret societies appear again in Europe. They inspire higher intuitive faculties in their members in the same way the old mysteries did. Members of these occult societies (I name but one, which is the most profound and important: that of the Rosicrucians, founded by Christian Rosenkreutz) embarked on a journey to the highest truths, as in the mysteries. We can observe their historical development up to the eighteenth century.[53]

Five months later, Rudolf Steiner presented the inner sphere of the Rosicrucian community for the first time to members of the Theosophical Society in a lecture titled "The Mystery of the Rosicrucians." The lecture focused on the Temple Legend and the Legend of the True Cross, and was part of Steiner's preparations for the second class of an esoteric school. About Christian Rosenkreutz and his Society of the Rosy Cross, Steiner said:

At the beginning of the fifteenth century a personality appeared in Europe who had been initiated into certain secrets in the East. It was Christian Rosenkreutz. Before the end of that incarnation, Christian Rosenkreutz initiated a number of individualities (no more than ten) into the mysteries in which he himself had been initiated, as far as that could be achieved with Europeans at the time. The small brotherhood (they called themselves the Brotherhood of the Rosy Cross, *Fraternitas Rosae Crucis*) broadcast a certain myth through a larger brotherhood that worked more exoterically.

At the time, Christian Rosenkreutz himself had revealed certain secrets in the innermost depths of the Rosicrucian mysteries, which could be grasped only by people who had undergone the necessary preparation. But, as I said, there were not more than ten in the small fraternity, and they were the real Rosicrucian initiates. What Christian Rosenkreutz taught could not be conveyed to many people, but was veiled in a kind of myth. Since its first origins in the early fifteenth century, that myth has been told and interpreted many times within the fraternities. It was told in the wider circle, but interpreted only in the smaller circle of those who had gained the necessary maturity.[54]

Christian Rosenkreutz therefore allowed the brotherhood to carry into the world the images of the Temple Legend and its references to Hiram Abiff, who represented an aspect of his own past. This brotherhood had the task of gradually bringing spiritual wisdom to civilization in preparation for future developments.

Shortly before he spoke about the "Mystery of the Rosicrucians" in a lecture in summer 1904, Rudolf Steiner had begun to publish his essays on esoteric training, "How Does One Attain Knowledge of Higher Worlds?" which had been wholly inspired by Christian Rosenkreutz. "What can be legitimately divulged [of the Rosicrucian path] to the public, I have described in the journal *Lucifer Gnosis*."[55] Two years later, in July 1906, Rudolf Steiner explained:

> The most suitable esoteric training for humanity today is Rosicrucianism, because it can accommodate scientific thinking. It was founded by Christian Rosenkreutz, the great individuality who has incarnated again and again since his initiation. Its teachings are the most liberal.... Teachers merely provide inspiration and counsel. But because of this freedom, pupils on that path are in greater danger of losing their mood of devotion, and of creating obstacles for themselves as a result. The teacher serves the pupil, whose devotion ought to be a free gift. Rosicrucian training today requires students to develop a particular kind of thinking, especially sense-free thinking. This is why I wrote *Philosophy of Freedom* and *Truth and Science*.[56]

Before the turn of the century Rudolf Steiner had provided a description, veiled as "idealist philosophy," of how to attain "sense-free thinking" and the state of consciousness that allowed for "intellectual inner vision."[57] The thread was continued in a different form in his *Theosophy*, and in the cosmology that had been announced in May 1904; it was published years later as *An Outline of Occult Science*. These works revealed the results of Rosicrucian spiritual research in micro- and macrocosmic terms: "the human being's innermost secrets in past, present, and future." The training that formed the foundation for this research had been initiated by Christian Rosenkreutz in Central Europe at the beginning of the modern era; "clearly defined, scientifically penetrated methods of initiation"[58] that are suited to the particular situation of "modern humanity."[59]

*

When Rudolf Steiner published *Theosophy* and his essays on inner development and started lecturing on Christian Rosenkreutz in 1904, he was well aware that the Theosophical Society had fallen away from its original path many years previously and was taking a different direction. The English theosophists who saw Steiner's Christian book on mysticism as the "true theosophy" were only a small minority. The Society's Indian center in Adyar had different goals. Steiner insisted that "the Rosicrucian methods will be the right methods of initiation into spiritual life for centuries to come."[60] In July 1906 he wrote in a personal letter to the president of the Theosophical Society, Annie Besant:

> Since the *fourteenth century,* the lines of occult activity have been clearly drawn in Central Europe; it is essential that we follow these directions.[61] [emphasis added]

At the time, Rudolf Steiner did not reveal anything more in his lectures about the "lines of occult activity" and their roots in the fourteenth century. Only very gradually did he give cautious indications here or there regarding the history of the original Rosicrucian community and their first writings. Their dissemination in the seventeenth century caused a tremendous stir. According to Steiner, nothing of the community's true history and contents had yet been divulged, because its members had committed themselves to firmly protect its inner space. In March 1907, he said in Berlin:

> If you take the works of Valentin Andreae and other Rosicrucian writings, you will not find anything special in them *unless you are familiar with the true foundation of Rosicrucianism.* Up to the present day it has not been possible to learn anything about the most elemental aspects of this spiritual stream, which has existed ever since the fourteenth century. What has found its way into the literature, what has been written and printed, are individual fragments that were lost and leaked to the public through betrayal. Because of charlatanry, corruption, foolishness, and stupidity they had become distorted and inaccurate. Since its inception, true, genuine Rosicrucianism has had only an oral tradition, and those who took part in it were sworn to secrecy. Nothing of great value has therefore entered public literature. One needs to know the elementary aspects of Rosicrucianism that (for certain reasons that cannot be explained within the scope of this lecture) can be made public now, and of which we will be able to speak today. We need to know them if we want to be able to make any sense of the often grotesque, often simply laughable, but rarely factual descriptions in literature.[62] [emphasis added]

But, not all of the information about the origin of the first brotherhood that has so far become known, mostly through Rosicrucian writings from the early seventeenth century, is necessarily false:

The basic tenor of the various communications is that, in the late fifteenth, early sixteenth century, Christian Rosenkreutz (not his true name, but the name under which he became known) traveled through the Orient where he learned about the book M.... The book, from which (so we are mysteriously informed) Paracelsus, the great medieval physician and mystic, drew his knowledge. This is indeed a fact, but only the initiates know: first, what the book M... is [*Liber Mundi*, the book of world knowledge]; and second, what it means to study the book M....[63]

Rudolf Steiner confirmed some elements of the popular reports, but decided not to disclose at that time any more facts concerning the beginnings of the brotherhood and the historical activities of the individuality of Christian Rosenkreutz. There is no doubt he knew about them, and that he had deeper insights into the Rosicrucian spiritual stream, which *"has existed ever since the fourteenth century."*

*

A few weeks after these presentations (of March 1907 in Berlin), following an intense period of preparation through lectures and writings, Rudolf Steiner made a resolute attempt to re-infuse the global Theosophical Society with original Rosicrucian spirituality, by reminding its members of the Society's spiritual origins. He had hoped and intended to do that right from the beginning ("...at the moment when we were called upon to unite with this theosophical movement, there was nothing else for it but to return to the original sources."[64]) As general secretary of the Theosophical Society's German Section, Rudolf Steiner had the task of organizing a major international congress in Munich. Destiny had provided the opportunity he had waited for. The program and admission tickets bore the Rose Cross as well as the three Rosicrucian mottoes from the *Fama*

E. D. N.
J. C. M.
P. S. S. R.

THEOSOPHISCHE GESELLSCHAFT

Foederation europäischer Sectionen

MÜNCHEN 1907.

Munich Congress 1907, program leaflet

Fraternitatis (abbreviated and adjusted[65]): *Ex Deo Nascimur — In Christo Morimur — Per Spiritum Sanctum Reviviscimus.* The congress venue in Munich was decorated like a *"true Rosicrucian temple"* (at the Kaim Auditorium, covered in red), and included initiation experiences of Christian Rosenkreutz from his incarnation as Lazarus-John, shaped by Rudolf Steiner into occult seals and columns (from the Book of Revelation). The seventh apocalyptic seal also bore the Rosicrucian mottoes. In his first lecture at the congress, Rudolf Steiner spoke about the "Initiation of the Rosicrucian," describing it as the extension of the Christian initiation, and the modern esoteric training that was necessary to perceive the spirit in matter.[66] It was the path that Rudolf Steiner himself had undoubtedly followed since his arrival in Vienna and his encounter with the two masters. In his second lecture at the congress ("Planetary and Human Evolution"), Steiner spoke about the microcosmic and macrocosmic insights "of the universal Rosicrucian spiritual stream," as presented in his book *Theosophy* and later in *Occult Science.* The metamorphosing capitals of the "Rosicrucian Temple" in the Kaim Auditorium represented the earth's planetary evolution.

Immediately after this major theosophical congress, Steiner gave a whole lecture cycle that was attended by a third (more than 200) of the congress members.[67] By concentrating on Rosicrucianism with such intensity, Rudolf Steiner tried, seven years before the outbreak of World War I, to awaken awareness in as many theosophists as possible of the "lines of occult activity that have been clearly drawn in Central Europe since the fourteenth century." There is reason to believe that he appealed to latent forces at a deeper destiny level, hoping to be able to make the original Rosicrucian impulse again the center of the society. On the stage of the auditorium he had placed the busts of Fichte, Schelling, and Hegel as representatives of the consciousness of "intellectual inner vision." "In Germany...the paths to this esoteric training have to proceed from the conceptual mysticism of Fichte, Schelling, and Hegel, whose actual esoteric foundations are not really understood."[68] Although Rudolf Steiner did not mention this explicitly, much depended on the success or failure of his enterprise. In his lecture cycle he also pointed out that it had been the "mission" of the Rosicrucian Brotherhood in the eighteenth century "to let something esoteric flow into the culture of Central Europe in a spiritual way."[69] As an example, he used the works of Lessing and Goethe. German idealism, as the preparation for a sustainable culture of the future and of peace in Central Europe, had consequently carried elements of Rosicrucian spirituality.

But a betrayal took place in the nineteenth century, according to Rudolf Steiner, "and caused certain ideas of Rosicrucian wisdom to leak out into the world exoterically."[70] As a result, Western culture had to remain without Rosicrucian influence for some time. The movement then necessarily faded into the background, "especially the great founder, who has always been on the physical plane since then."[71] Rudolf Steiner did not offer detailed explanations for the withdrawal; nor did he elaborate on its consequences, which include the one-sided, unrestrained activity of materialist-technological forces.[72] The impression emerged, nevertheless, that future development strongly depends on the successful infusion of a new Rosicrucian spirituality into Europe at the present time.

It is unlikely that the impulse for the 1907 initiative had come from Rudolf Steiner alone. It certainly involved his masters. The Munich Congress was, however, not destined to constitute a major breakthrough. The Theosophical Society and its spiritual science did not evolve as potent cultural factors in Europe in the following years. In 1924 when he looked back, Rudolf Steiner said to Ita Wegman in Paris that World War I could have been prevented, if it had been possible in the first decade of the twentieth century to establish theosophy as a Rosicrucian anthroposophy in Central Europe, and in France in particular.[73]

*

In Munich, Rudolf Steiner outlined the anthropological and cosmological content of "Theosophy of the Rosicrucian," emphasizing that these were research results that were accessible to thinking, and compatible with modern natural science. He described Rosicrucian wisdom as being oriented toward practical life. Modern Rosicrucian spiritual science could "be put to use in practical life" and be "instrumental in creating the culture of the future":

> Rosicrucian wisdom must not stream just into our heads and hearts, but also into our hands; into our manual skills, into what we do in everyday life. It is not about sentimental sympathy, but about striving toward doing what is good for humanity. Imagine a society that preaches only human brotherhood. That would not be Rosicrucian, because the Rosicrucian would say, "Imagine a person lying in the road with a broken leg. If fourteen people stand around him feeling sorry for him, but none of them can deal with the broken leg, these fourteen are less important than the one who might not be sentimental, but who knows how to deal with the broken leg and does it." That is the attitude of the Rosicrucian. What counts is practical knowledge; the possibility to know what needs doing. Too much talk of sympathy is even seen as a danger by Rosicrucians, since it has an element of astral sensuality. Sensuality on the physical plane corresponds to a permanent longing for feeling rather than knowing on the astral plane. Practical knowledge not based on materialism, but on spiritual insight, enables us to take action in life. Harmony flows from the necessary insight that the world must move forward; and it flows the more reliably if we gain knowledge. We can say of the one who knows how to deal with a broken leg that if he is no philanthropist he might not care about the sufferer. That would be possible if physical knowledge alone were involved. It would not be possible with spiritual knowledge.

There is no spiritual knowledge that does not inspire practical actions in life.[74]

His essay *The Education of the Child in the Light of Spiritual Science*, which was published in the same year, 1907, was therefore described by Rudolf Steiner as Rosicrucian. ("You will realize how practical the effect of theosophy can be if you read my little book *The Education of the Child in the Light of Spiritual Science*. What I wrote there cannot be known without Rosicrucian theosophy. It must not remain theory, but become part of practical daily life."[75])

*

Around the time of the Munich Congress, Rudolf Steiner introduced radical changes to the Esoteric School that he led as part of the Theosophical Society's German Section.[76] Because the Theosophical Society and Annie Besant's esoteric leadership showed severe signs of decline and because Steiner's conversations with Besant during the congress had failed, he removed the school from its former context. In doing so, he separated it from the "Masters of the East" who had been its spiritual leaders since Blavatsky had founded the "Esoteric School of the Theosophical Society" in 1888. For three years leading up to the Munich Congress, Rudolf Steiner had done all he could to preserve the school's spiritual ties with the East. Now he had to accept that this was no longer possible, and he had to act accordingly. His decision was presumably preceded by particular events in the sphere of the masters.[77] When the esoteric schools were separated, he said to the members of his school, on May 28, 1907, in Munich:

> Until now both schools were united in a wide circle under the masters' joint leadership. The Western school has become independent and from now on two equivalent schools will exist: one in the East and the other in the West;

two smaller circles instead of the one big one. The Eastern school is led by Mrs. Annie Besant, and those who feel drawn to it in their hearts cannot remain in our school. You must listen carefully to your heart to find out which way you are drawn. Our Western school is guided by two masters: Master Jesus and Master Christian Rosenkreutz. They lead us on two paths: the Christian path and the Christian-Rosicrucian path. The Great White Lodge guides all spiritual movements, and Master Jesus and Master Christian Rosenkreutz are part of it.[78]

Three days later he continued these considerations:

The Western school used to be affiliated and subordinated to the Eastern school. Now they are connected fraternally but go their own ways. The Western school is no longer subordinated, but coordinated with the Eastern school. What I teach on behalf of the Masters of the West stands independently beside Mrs. Besant's teachings on behalf of the Masters of the East.

The Christian esoteric training and the Christian-Rosicrucian esoteric training will from now on exist in the West. The former teaches through the heart, the latter through the head.[79]

Rudolf Steiner placed the esoteric school over which he presided under the leadership of only two masters. They had both been crucial in his own development and were *de facto* the spiritual leaders of the West.[80]

*

Three months later Rudolf Steiner threw light on the wider historical context of his decision (a decision that had arisen

from the struggle about the future of the Theosophical Society
and its esoteric center) when he wrote to the French theosophist
Edouard Schuré:

> Whether [the Theosophical Society] will continue to
> thrive in the West depends entirely on its ability to
> embrace the principle of Western initiation. Eastern ini-
> tiations must necessarily ignore the *Christ principle* as
> the central *cosmic* factor of evolution. But without that
> principle, the theosophical movement will not be able to
> govern the cultures of the West, which are rooted in the
> life of Christ. The revelations of Eastern initiation would
> have to stand as sects *beside* the living culture of the West.
> They could hope for a successful evolution only if they
> eradicated the Christ principle from Western culture. That
> would be the same as eradicating the *true meaning of the
> earth*, which lies in the knowledge and realization of the
> intentions of the *living Christ*. To unveil these intentions
> in full wisdom, beauty, and deed is the highest endeavor
> of Rosicrucianism. Studying Eastern wisdom is a highly
> valuable enterprise, because the peoples of the West have
> lost their understanding of esotericism, while the peoples
> of the East have retained theirs. The right esotericism to be
> *introduced* in the West must be the Rosicrucian-Christian
> esotericism, because it has given birth to Western life; and
> if it were lost, humanity on earth would repudiate its own
> purpose and destiny. It is within this esotericism alone
> that harmony of science and religion can blossom ....[81]
> [author's emphasis]

For the first time, Rudolf Steiner brought the Theosophical
Society together with the destiny of Christianity. The "Christ
principle," he said, lives as a "central cosmic factor" in the initiation of Christian Rosenkreutz and Master Jesus. Steiner's
"having stood spiritually before the Mystery of Golgotha in a

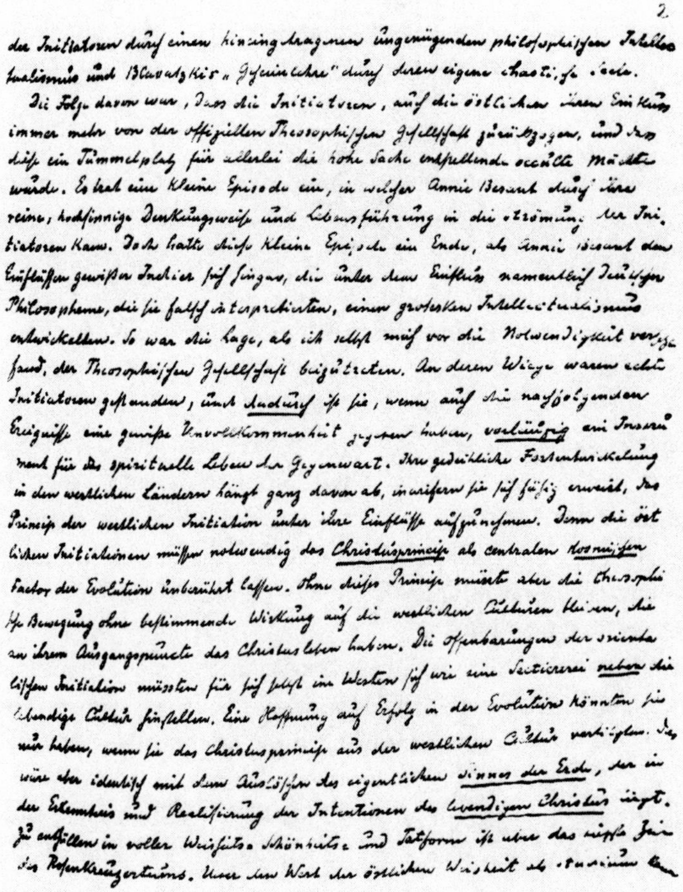

2.

der Initiatoren durch einen hineingetragenen ungenügenden philosophischen Intellectualismus und Blavatskys „Geheimlehre" durch deren eigene chaotische Seele.

Die Folge davon war, daß die Initiatoren, auch die östlichen, ihren Einfluß immer mehr von der offiziellen Theosophischen Gesellschaft zurückzogen, und daß diese ein Tummelplatz für allerlei die hohe Sache entstellende occulte Mächte wurde. Es trat eine kleine Episode ein, in welcher Annie Besant durch ihre reine, hochsinnige Denkungsweise und Lebensführung in die Strömung der Initiatoren kam. Doch hatte diese kleine Episode ein Ende, als Annie Besant den Einflüssen gewisser Inder sich hingab, die unter dem Einfluß namentlich deutscher Philosopheme, die sie falsch interpretierten, einen grotesken Intellectualismus entwickelten. So war die Lage, als ich selbst mich vor die Notwendigkeit versetzt fand, der Theosophischen Gesellschaft beizutreten. An deren Wiege waren echte Initiatoren gestanden, und dadurch ist sie, wenn auch die nachfolgenden Ereignisse eine gewisse Unvollkommenheit gegeben haben, vorläufig ein Instrument für das spirituelle Leben der Gegenwart. Ihre gedeihliche Fortentwickelung in den westlichen Ländern hängt ganz davon ab, inwiefern sie sich fähig erweist, das Princip der westlichen Initiation unter ihre Einflüsse aufzunehmen. Denn die östlichen Initiationen müssen notwendig das Christusprincip als centralen kosmischen Factor der Evolution unberührt lassen. Ohne dieses Princip müßte aber die theosophische Bewegung ohne bestimmende Wirkung auf die westlichen Culturen bleiben, die an ihrem Ausgangspunkte das Christusleben haben. Die Offenbarungen der orientalischen Initiation müßten für sich selbst im Westen sich wie eine Sectirerei neben die lebendige Cultur hinstellen. Eine Hoffnung auf Erfolg in der Evolution könnten sie nur haben, wenn sie das Christusprincip aus der westlichen Cultur vertilgten. Das wäre aber identisch mit dem Auslöschen des eigentlichen Sinnes der Erde, der in der Erkenntnis und Realisierung der Intentionen des lebendigen Christus liegt. Zu enthüllen in voller Weisheits-, Schönheits- und Tatform ist aber das nächste Ziel des Rosenkreuzertums. Ueber den Wert der östlichen Weisheit als Studium kann

Rudolf Steiner's notes for Edouard Schuré. 1907, p. 2.
Rudolf Steiner Archives, Dornach

deep and solemn celebration of knowledge" meant just that.
The question was whether the Theosophical Society would find
its way back to the principle of the Western masters who had
inspired its foundation in 1875; and whether it would be able to
contribute actively to the preparation for the etheric reappearance of the Christ.

In various lectures from 1908 onward, Rudolf Steiner described
that preparation as the Theosophical Society's true task and the
justification of its existence ("We realize that theosophy places
tremendous responsibility on us, since it expects us to prepare
for the actual event of Christ's reappearance."[82]) "Knowledge
and realization of the intentions of the *living Christ*" also means
that we know of and prepare for his reappearance as a central
factor in future evolution.[83] In Steiner's notes for Schuré, he
described as the "highest endeavor" of Rosicrucianism, the revelation of "these intentions in wisdom, beauty, and deed." He
had himself in Munich given an example of what was meant by
that: through the wisdom of his lectures, the artistic beauty of
the congress venue, and the emphasis he placed on the will element of "practical life."

In his notes to Schuré, Steiner wrote further about Christian
Rosenkreutz and the historical origin of the Rosicrucian stream,
as well as about a crucial moment in the nineteenth century:

> In the first half of the fifteenth century, Christian
> Rosenkreutz traveled to the East in order to find the bal-
> ance between Eastern and Western initiations. As a result
> he *firmly* established the Rosicrucian approach in the West
> after his return. Rosicrucianism would be the strictly secret
> school for the preparation of what was to be the task of
> esotericism around the turn of the twentieth century, when
> the exoteric natural sciences would have found the pre-
> liminary solution to certain problems.
> According to Christian Rosenkreutz these were: 1) The
> invention of spectroscopy, which revealed the material

composition of the cosmos. 2) The introduction of material evolution into organic science. 3) The acknowledgment of the fact that there was a state of consciousness other than the ordinary one, based on the recognition of hypnosis and suggestion.

These material insights had to reach a certain maturity in the sciences before some of the Rosicrucian principles could cease to be secret knowledge, and become public information.[84] [author's emphasis]

Rudolf Steiner pointed out for the first time that Christian Rosenkreutz had in fact traveled to the East, but also that the occult purpose for his journey had been *"to find the balance between Eastern and Western initiations."* The attempt to find a balance repeated itself in the constellation of occult powers in the Theosophical Society at the beginning of the twentieth century (which is why, although it was a burden to him, Rudolf Steiner agreed only quite late and against his will to the total separation from the Theosophical Society and its Eastern orientation. (*"I will not call it [the separation] an ordeal just to avoid being called sentimental."*[85])

According to Rudolf Steiner, Christian Rosenkreutz, after his return from the East, founded the Rosicrucian school in the West as a "strictly secret" institution. Its spiritual pupils actively prepared for the time when esoteric knowledge would become public knowledge; that is, when the natural sciences would have evolved to a particular level. That level was indeed reached in the second half of the nineteenth century in all three fields named by Christian Rosenkreutz. It was now possible for "certain Rosicrucian principles to cease to be secret knowledge, and become public information." The Theosophical Society had decided in 1875 to take on that task, but it soon lost sight of the Rosicrucian inspiration that formed its spiritual basis.

Rudolf Steiner indicated during an esoteric lesson in Berlin, shortly after his return from Barr (Alsace, France, October 9,

1907), that the spiritual goal that the Rosicrucians worked toward and prepared for was the new Michael Age, which began in the year 1879. In the same context, he placed the beginning of the Rosicrucian movement exactly in the middle of the thirteenth century, mentioning the year 1250. "In 1250 a spiritual stream emerged that reached its climax in 1459 when Christian Rosenkreutz was appointed a Knight of the Rosy Cross. Then (in 1510) began the era that in occultism is called the Gabriel Age. 1879 was the beginning of the Michael Age....."[86]

*

At the end of 1907, three months after he wrote down the "Documents de Barr" for Edouard Schuré, Rudolf Steiner spoke again about Christian Rosenkreutz, at the Düsseldorf branch of the Theosophical Society. He said about the initiation of Rosenkreutz just after the middle of the fifteenth century, "In 1459, the true founder of the Rosicrucian stream reached the stage where he was granted the power to carry that initiation into the world."[87] In his notes for Schuré from autumn 1907, Steiner had also referred to the event of 1459, emphasizing Christian Rosenkreutz' initiation through Mani at that time (Mani possessed true knowledge of the mission of evil.[88])

In Düsseldorf, Steiner also mentioned that Christian Rosenkreutz had "returned again and again" since 1459 as leader of the Rosicrucian stream and initiation, "living his life 'in the same body' through the centuries."[89] In his Munich Whitsun lectures "Theosophy of the Rosicrucian," Steiner had also remarked on Rosenkreutz' incarnating in every century, describing him as the "great founder" of the Rosicrucian stream "who since that time has always been on the physical plane," until a certain (temporary) withdrawal occurred in the nineteenth century.[90] In Düsseldorf, Steiner also hinted at the "close restriction" of the Rosicrucian school and its methods through the centuries, saying, in accordance with his Munich presentations, that it was "known only to a closed circle, strictly closed off in the nineteenth (the most materialistic) century."[91] An important change took place in the last third of the nineteenth century, when conditions in the natural sciences had evolved, as outlined by Steiner in the Barr documents. The necessity arose "for theosophy to reveal to the world at least the most elementary aspects of what had been taught in the Rosicrucian schools."[92]

*

Following his brief references of 1906/07 (when he had mentioned the fourteenth century and 1250), Rudolf Steiner did not reveal more details about the pre-1459 activities of Christian Rosenkreutz. He merely indicated, without further elaboration (in the summer of 1909 in Budapest, Hungary) that the Rosicrucian community had been initially active *"in the thirteenth and fourteenth centuries."*[93] Two years earlier, in the esoteric lesson of June 1, 1907, in Munich, he had explained that "in the thirteenth and fourteenth centuries" Rosenkreutz had undertaken the great mission of *"merging the spiritual culture of the East with that of the West."*[94] Steiner did not disclose on this occasion whether Rosenkreutz' eastern journey "in the first half of the fifteenth century" with the aim of finding "the balance between Eastern and Western initiations" (Barr documents) in fact concluded what he had attempted for some time (nor what the attempt actually consisted of). The Rosicrucian theme faded into the background in Steiner's lectures of 1908, 1909, and 1910. After the intense attention he had devoted to it in the years before, Steiner continued, nonetheless, to introduce important aspects of the Rosicrucian stream, such as the fact that preparations for its esoteric movement had started as early as the fourth century A.D.[95] The *content* of Steiner's major lecture cycles of those years and his Christological book *Occult Science* (completed in 1999 and published in early 1910)

were intimately connected with Christian Rosenkreutz and his
school,[96] as was the mystery drama *The Portal of Initiation* that
was first performed in Munich in summer 1910 (three years
after the Whitsun Congress that had served as a preparation for
it). Steiner explicitly referred to the play as a "Rosicrucian mystery," saying it had been written down and performed "through"
him.[97] Most members of the Theosophical Society and of the
audience were not really aware of these circumstances. Many
elements were still missing, so full comprehension of Christian
Rosenkreutz and the "lines of occult activity" that had been at
work "since the fourteenth century" was not yet possible.

*

The situation changed abruptly just before Michaelmas 1911,
when Steiner spoke for the first time directly and in detail about
Christian Rosenkreutz and his community. That happened in the
Swiss town of Neuchâtel on September 27 and 28, 1911, after
Annie Besant had (unexpectedly and on short notice) cancelled
a theosophical congress in Genoa.[98] Rudolf Steiner had been lecturing on Christology in Lugano, Locarno, and Milan. He introduced the first lecture in Neuchâtel with the words: *"It fills me
with deep satisfaction to visit for the first time this newly founded
branch, which bears the sublime name of Christian Rosenkreutz.
It gives me the opportunity to speak about Christian Rosenkreutz
for the first time in more detail."*[99] Steiner seemed to imply that
the opportunity arose for the first time because the new branch
in Neuchâtel was named after, or rather consecrated to Christian
Rosenkreutz. The friends of anthroposophy in Neuchâtel had
approached him with their wish or request for more intimate
instruction. They felt the need "to become better acquainted
with the various incarnations and the particular essence of the
greatest teacher of Christianity, Christian Rosenkreutz."[100]
    At other anthroposophic branches (especially Munich,
Stuttgart, Cassel, Vienna, and Hamburg, during the months that

Rudolf Steiner, 1911

followed, Rudolf Steiner continued to elaborate on what he had begun in Neuchâtel.[101]) The initial two lectures in Neuchâtel, given before Michaelmas, were, however, unique in their intensity and substance. It is likely that Rudolf Steiner had known for a long time what he related there, but that he had chosen to keep it to himself. For the first time now, he devoted two lectures specifically to the individuality of Christian Rosenkreutz. On the following day, Michaelmas day, he visited Einsiedeln, the birth place of the physician Paracelsus.[102]

In Neuchâtel, Rudolf Steiner began his historical descriptions with the middle of the thirteenth century, a period that he characterized as a time of immense spiritual darkness, when all access to spiritual insights was temporarily interrupted; even initiates retained only memories of such insights. When that period of preparation for the dawning intellectual culture came to a close,[103] twelve important personalities met somewhere in Europe (in a place "of which it is not yet possible to speak; but speaking of it will be possible in the not too distant future."[104]) They carried within themselves the entire Atlantean and post-Atlantean wisdom, and also all the present intellectual knowledge. "The whole of spiritual life was open to these twelve personalities."[105] Rudolf Steiner spoke of twelve views of the world,[106] which were represented by the "council of wise men," and which were reflected in each other. Each of the wise men lived in full awareness of his spiritual task. According to Rudolf Steiner all of them were "knowledgeable, quiet, harmonious spirits," who were imbued with Christianity, although they rejected its ecclesiastical manifestation, a fact that was known to those around them. "They were permeated with the greatness of Christianity, but to the outside world they seemed to be its enemies."[107]

The "council of the twelve" turned to the education of a child for whose birth it had been prepared for a long time.[108] "It was known to the council of the twelve wise men that a boy would be born in that era who had lived in Palestine at the time of the Christ event; a boy who had been present at the Mystery of Golgotha ... ."[109] Rudolf Steiner explained:

> The thirteenth had been announced in a way that was extraordinary for the twelve clairvoyant wise men. When the spiritual darkness [of the mid-thirteenth century] was over and the first light of clairvoyance could radiate out, they knew that a child would be born who had experienced important and remarkable incarnations. They knew above all that one of those incarnations had taken place at the time of the Mystery of Golgotha.[110]

The thirteenth was in fact the individuality that at the "turning point of time" had been awakened by Christ as Lazarus and had become his disciple John. He had been close to Christ's heart, and later he had stood beneath the cross of Golgotha with Mary.[111] In the following centuries, the individuality, who had been chosen for a special task for humanity, had continued to develop heart forces of devotion and love in less prominent incarnations, and returned to the earth to live piously and with reverence. "He [the thirteenth] was a great soul, a pious, deeply mystical individual who had been born with these qualities...."[112] The education of the thirteenth was, as had long been ordained,[113] reserved entirely to the personalities who belonged to the "council of the twelve wise men." The child was taken to them, at a particular place in Europe, away from the environment into which he had been born. "Separated from the exoteric outer world, the child lived solely under their influence. They were his educators, who also cared for his body."[114] "They brought him up with the utmost care..."[115] Rudolf Steiner pointed out repeatedly that it was a *unique* process in the history of the world and of consciousness, and that it took place at a special time.[116] In regard to the objectives and methods of the education through the "wise men" he said:

It was their endeavor to unite the various religions into
one; and they were convinced that their twelve streams
constitute the whole of spiritual life. Each of them exerted
his particular influence on the child. Their aim was to
achieve a synthesis of all the religions, and they knew that
this aim could not be accomplished through theories but
only through a spiritual life. It was therefore essential for
the thirteenth to be educated in the right way.[117]

The twelve were certainly not fanatics, and they kept all
theoretical teaching from the boy. They shared their lives
with him; and in this way the twelve different rays of light
passed from them into the boy, and his soul received them
in harmony. It would not have been possible to examine
him in the usual way, but in his mind and soul lived, transformed into feeling and sensation, what had radiated into
his soul from the bearers of the twelve different types of
religion. His entire soul mood was a harmonious resonance of the twelve creeds of humanity that are spread
across the earth.[118]

As a consequence of this "soul mood," the soul's relationship
to the body changed; "and remarkably, the wider and more harmonious the boy's inner soul-life grew, the more delicate his body
became; more and more delicate."[119] Rudolf Steiner said that the
spiritual power of the thirteenth continued to grow "infinitely,"
while his physical strength drained away. He lost almost all connection with the external world and all interest in the physical
world. "He lived only for the spiritual development for which
he received inspiration from the twelve."[120] While the initiation
proceeded, the thirteenth (who had by now grown into a youth)
rejected all physical sustenance. As a result[121] his body became
wholly transparent ("a shining, brilliant spirit in a transparent
body."[122]) After that he seemed as though dead for some days,
while the twelve were around him to guide him: "they let their

wisdom flow into the thirteenth in short formulas that were like reverent prayers, while the thirteenth lay as though dead."[123] Then a great transformation occurred:

> Now the youth was inwardly transformed. The twelve different streams of human wisdom were like one light; and he spoke out tremendous and most wonderful secrets. He did not say what the first, the second, the third said. In an entirely new form and in a wonderful way, he expressed what all of them would say together: the combined knowledge of all twelve of them. He pronounced this wisdom as if it had only just been born within him, as if a higher spirit had spoken in him; and each of the twelve was able to learn something new. And they all learned from him. They were offered infinite wisdom; each of them received a more perfect explanation of what he knew from before.[124]

For weeks the newly awakened youth reproduced the wisdom of the twelve wise men in a new, imaginative form.[125] "The new form was as though given by Christ himself."[126] The wise men called the new form of knowledge "true Christianity" and the "synthesis" of all religions. With their initiation they had worked for a long time persistently toward this synthesis (at least since the fourth century[127]): "The twelve now felt: only now have we received the twelve religions and streams of wisdom as one coherent whole! In them lived from then on what we call Rosicrucian Christianity."[128]

"Rosicrucian Christianity" as the rebirth of old wisdom was not only Christ-oriented and "as though given by Christ himself." The reawakened youth also spoke of an actual meeting with the Christ. "The twelve realized that the youth had been through a Damascus experience, a repetition of the vision that Paul had on the road to Damascus."[129] He explained the Pauline event to them also in a "higher sense." His transparent physical body had been revived; its death-like state was overcome.

In a lecture about the working of "spiritual economy" in human evolution on March 28, 1909, Rudolf Steiner had indicated that, since the beginning of the modern era, "imprints" of the "I" of Christ weave themselves into individual advanced personalities. "Since the sixteenth century, imprints of the Christ-I have been ready to weave themselves into the "I" of certain individualities. Christian Rosenkreutz, the first Rosicrucian, was one of these individualities. It is due to this development that a more intimate relationship with the Christ has become possible, as revealed by esoteric knowledge."[130] Rudolf Steiner spoke of a process that had started in the sixteenth century, three centuries after the initiation of the youth within the council of the "wise men." His transformation still bore obvious signs of this process. "Resurrection and life" entered into the deathlike body, penetrated the soul, and enlivened the body with the power of the "phantom," the resurrected body of the Christ.[131]

As Lazarus-John, his individuality had once been called back to life through Christ's power of initiation ("Lazarus, come forth!"). Now, twelve centuries later, a further stage of his encounter with and penetration through the Christ took place.

The "first school" of Rosicrucian Christianity began with the transformation and return of the "youth." After the school had been founded through the education by the twelve, the individuality that had lived in the child and in the youth soon withdrew to the spiritual world. According to Steiner, the "thirteenth died relatively young."[132] His etheric body, which contained the Christ-permeated mystery wisdom, did not dissolve entirely, but remained in the earth spirit atmosphere from where he continued to inspire the twelve and their pupils (*"so that the Rosicrucian occult stream could radiate out from them"*[133]).

Christian Rosenkreutz reincarnated in 1378, around a hundred years after his previous incarnation. We know from Rudolf Steiner that his ether body was illumined and irradiated from the spiritual world by his former, Christ-permeated ether body. As in his thirteenth-century incarnation, Rosenkreutz grew up "in a special way" among the pupils and successors of the twelve, but not in such seclusion from the world as had been required during his initiation.

When he had reached the end of his fourth seven-year period, at the age of twenty-eight, his etheric body guided him to the East so that he would "relive the event of Damascus."[134] He remained in the East for seven years, absorbing the entire wisdom of his time. His journeys probably extended even further than the early seventeenth century description in the *Fama Fraternitatis* suggests. According to Rudolf Steiner, he traveled "the entire Western world and *almost all parts of the earth known at the time*, seeking to absorb anew all the wisdom he had received in earlier lives in order to instill it, like an essence, into the culture of his time."[135]

After his return to Europe in 1413, at the beginning of the fifth post-Atlantean era, Christian Rosenkreutz admitted the most advanced pupils and followers of the twelve into his school, and became their teacher. It was then that the Rosicrucians began to work actively, as an esoteric community, on the prevailing culture and civilization.[136] Then, and for many centuries to come, most of the work of the Rosicrucians entailed "sacred natural science,"[137] and alchemy in particular. Alchemy included the transformation of human soul forces through sacrificial service.[138] Everything the community produced had to be offered as a gift. As the Rosicrucian fraternity grew, the work of its members took on a more therapeutic quality as they worked mostly as physicians:

> Those who were gathered by the first Rosicrucians into a wider brotherhood appeared here and there in the world. They tended not to be well-known personalities, but physicians or healers who disseminated their wisdom while carrying out their healing profession.[139]

They did not propagate any theories, concepts, ideas, or knowledge, but performed practical tasks with the aim of furthering human civilization and infusing people, almost unnoticeably, with wisdom.[140]

The Rosicrucian school and brotherhood was an "institution of spiritual research and spiritual knowledge."[141] Its achievements were beneficial to the world, although the school itself remained concealed.

In his fourteenth-century incarnation, which led him to the East, Christian Rosenkreutz lived to be more than a hundred years old. In 1459, at quite an advanced age, he was initiated by Mani in an event that represented the Rosicrucian stream's spiritual zenith.[142] The initiation was necessary for Rosenkreutz to advance to a level that would bestow on him "the power to carry that initiation into the world."[143] While the Rosicrucians had been culturally active before, it needed the event of 1459 for the initiation principle to be brought to humanity as a modern path of inner development. Rosicrucian initiation had, and still has, the task of establishing the conscious connection between the human "I" and the Christ-I, as in the Pauline Damascus experience, which Christian Rosenkreutz absorbed in order to make it accessible to humankind.

*

In Neuchâtel as well as in other places, Rudolf Steiner pointed out that Christian Rosenkreutz works through his Christ-permeated ether body. This ether body has grown ever stronger and ever more powerful because of the spiritual work achieved by the Rosicrucian community. Rosenkreutz' spiritual life (or love) body also inspires the modern spiritual sciences of theosophy or anthroposophy:

Theosophy is nurtured by the etheric body of Christian Rosenkreutz, and theosophists allow themselves to be overshadowed by his etheric body. It inspires them, whether or not Christian Rosenkreutz is incarnated.[144]

When Rudolf Steiner said those words, Christian Rosenkreutz was incarnated.[145] But his influence extends beyond his individual incarnations, and is related to spiritual science and its future tasks. *Only* the anthroposophic (not the Eastern) path of inner development makes it possible to connect with the Christ-permeated ether body of Christian Rosenkreutz. In the lectures on Christ's reappearance in the etheric, which Rudolf Steiner began in January 1910, he spoke of the future when many people would experience the Pauline Damascus event (which Christian Rosenkreutz replicated spiritually in the thirteenth century, and sought again in the fourteenth). The experience would manifest as "natural" etheric clairvoyance, independently of any esoteric school, and would bring about a union of the different religions.[146] According to Steiner, this would be possible because of the active spiritual form of Christian Rosenkreutz, his Christ-permeated ether body, which works through his pupils:[147]

Devotion to the powerful etheric body of Christian Rosenkreutz will bring us a new clairvoyance and reveal sublime spiritual powers, but only if we follow Christian Rosenkreutz' path of inner development. Until now, an esoteric Rosicrucian preparation was required for this. But it is the mission of the twentieth century to make that etheric body grow sufficiently powerful to work exoterically. If we allow ourselves to be imbued by it, we will see what Paul saw on the road to Damascus. Although the influence of Christian Rosenkreutz' etheric body formerly was felt only within the Rosicrucian school, it will be experienced by more and more people in the twentieth century, and they will come to perceive Christ's appearance in an etheric body. It is the work of the Rosicrucians that makes the etheric vision of the Christ possible. The number of people able to perceive it will grow and grow. We owe this reappearance to the important work of the Twelve and the Thirteenth in the thirteenth and fourteenth centuries.[148]

The fact that Rudolf Steiner separated his esoteric school from that of Theosophy, placing it under the sole influence of Christian Rosenkreutz and Master Jesus, was intimately connected with those events. The search for a physically incarnated Christ (as pursued at Adyar, the Theosophical Society's center in India) and the supposed finding of that incarnation in the Hindu boy Jiddu Krishnamurti was not only a serious mistake, it also threatened to prevent or halt the esoteric future impulses connected with Christian Rosenkreutz in relation to the etheric reappearance of Christ. Spiritual students were to be supported or "over-shadowed" in the future by the Christ-imbued etheric body of Christian Rosenkreutz, and not by anything else. In 1908, when the esoteric school had become independent, and was placed wholly under the influence of Christian Rosenkreutz and Master Jesus, Rudolf Steiner began his extensive lecture courses on the Gospels. In 1909 he said, referring to those lectures and their background:

> The words of the Gospels are being increasingly misunder-stood. People try to read things into them, and examine them with the methods of exoteric history. But exoteric history must remain silent for a while when one carries out spiritual research. We need to take the words of the Gospels literally again, because it is in their literal meaning that their true wisdom is revealed! From the spiritual world we were told to learn to understand the literal meaning of the Gospels again. From that impulse, from its expansion and development, grew everything we tried to achieve with our study of the Gospels of John, Luke, and Matthew; and what we will still try to explore with the Gospel of Mark. We must try to return to a literal understanding of the

Gospels! *Those whose impulses we receive from the spiritual world tell us that.* That is the future Christianity: to follow the impulse of understanding the literal meaning of the Gospels.[149]

Two years later, Steiner's Neuchâtel lectures revealed why humanity owes its spiritual future to Christian Rosenkreutz; to his essence, his path, and his sacrifice. From early on, the Rosicrucian movement had conducted its scientific research in the etheric sphere. Humanity's increasing orientation toward the etheric life, which has been prepared by the Rosicrucians, would from the twentieth century and with the help of Michael[150] allow an ever-growing number of people to perceive the Christ in that sphere, in Christ's etheric body. ("The Christ will reappear because human beings will rise up to him in their etheric vision."[151]) When addressing the Rosenkreutz branch, Steiner underlined Christian Rosenkreutz' importance for the continuation of the anthroposophic movement, and his ability to give support and strength, which Steiner knew from experience. He concluded these lectures, just before Michaelmas 1911, with the words:

> We will know Christian Rosenkreutz if we enter deeply into his individuality, and gain awareness of the fact that his spirit will continue to be there. The closer we come to this great spirit, the stronger we will grow. The etheric body of this great leader, who will always be there, can give us much strength and support, if we appeal to him for help.
>
> I myself will continue to call attention to this important, promising task of ours, and ask the great leader of the West to grant us his help.[152]

The Gospel lectures, which had begun prior to the Neuchâtel lectures (and concluded in Basel in 1912), were also imbued with "strength and support" from Christian Rosenkreutz, and served to prepare the Christological development of the twentieth century and of the future. But the impulse for the lectures had come not only from Christian Rosenkreutz ("those whose impulses we receive from the spiritual world"). *Master Jesus*, who inspired the Christian-esoteric schools, and who was the "greatest helper of all who strive to understand the important event of Palestine," was also clearly connected very intimately with Rudolf Steiner's Gospel lectures. His whole essence and activity, his Christ-imbued spirituality, were crucial also to Christian Rosenkreutz.[153] At the end of his lecture on the spiritual preparation of the Rosicrucian movement in the fourth century, delivered in Munich on August 31, 1909, Rudolf Steiner pointed out: "The striving spiritual scientist of today needs to meet the two fundamental requirements that can further human spiritual development. Deep permeation with the life of Christ is the first element; a spiritual cosmology that will enhance the understanding of the Christ is the second. The life of Christ in the depths of the heart and an understanding of the world that will engender an understanding of Christ, these will be the two elements."[154] *"The life of Christ in the depths of the heart"* was closely linked to the essence of Master Jesus. It had determined Christian mysticism during the late Middle Ages and the dawn of modernism, just as spiritual cosmology had been part of the original teachings of the Rosicrucian schools. The "life of Christ in the depths of the heart"—the entering of the Christ impulse into the innermost depths of the individuality—continued to be highly relevant for the future of humanity, but needed to be transformed to include "I" awareness and conscious selflessness to make it better suited to the modern age (*"Not with the powers of the intellect, but with our innermost powers of soul and heart, we must take hold of the Christ impulse."*)[155] Steiner's courses on the Gospels, which culminated in the Fifth Gospel, originated in the sun-sphere of the heart, which is connected with Master Jesus. Rudolf Steiner worked out of that sphere. He once wrote in his notebook:

Feeling the need for YOUR grace,
Christ-light of the world, I await
      the powers
      of YOUR enlightenment
      that unlock the portals of the soul
With inner serenity I will
thank YOU for YOUR gift
and present it
as YOUR gift to humanity
Instrument OF YOUR WORD
Will I be
with my soul's
      best powers
      truest depths
      serenest reverence.[156]

*

At the end of 1911, three months after the Neuchâtel lectures
and the subsequent related Christological presentations in Basel
(on the etherization of the blood and the reappearance of the
Christ[157]) and Karlsruhe (*From Jesus to Christ* [158]), Rudolf
Steiner informed the members of the Anthroposophical Society
of the foundation of a "Society for Theosophical Art and Way
of Living." The *foundation*[159] was directly inspired, as Rudolf
Steiner said, by the individuality we have referred to "since
ancient times in the West as Christian Rosenkreutz."[160] The foundation was under the direct protection of Christian Rosenkreutz,
and was established in response to an appeal from the spiritual world—an appeal to initiate a new way of working.[161] The
foundation was to become increasingly prominent in the world.
Only one of its "sections" would relate to the arts: "What we
were able to establish so far relates to the one section, to the one
branch of this foundation that is devoted to the artistic representation of Rosicrucian occultism."[162]

Im Gefühle der Bedürftigkeit DEINER Gnade,
Christus-Licht der Welt, harre ich
     nach Kräften
     öffnend der Seele Pforten

     DEINER Erleuchtung
Still in mir will ich sein
und DIR danken DEINER Gabe
und sie geben
als DEIN Geschenk an Menschen
Werkzeug DEINES Wortes
will ich sein
mit meiner Seele
     besten Kräften
     echten Tiefen
     stillsten Erfurchten.

From Rudolf Steiner's notebook

Rudolf Steiner's mystery dramas, the Munich impulse to erect a "Johannes building," and the columned ritual room at the Stuttgart branch were all representations of the "artistic stream of Rosicrucian occultism." Their task was to offset "the Ahrimanic influences on the physical plane."[163] With a small number of supporters, Rudolf Steiner worked actively in those years to make visible the formative principles of an anthroposophically inspired approach to the arts and "unveil the intentions of the living Christ in wisdom, beauty, and deed." According to what Steiner wrote in Barr in 1907, this was the "highest endeavor of Rosicrucianism."

After 1910, through the years when anthroposophy was established, Steiner presented his ideas primarily in lectures and writings as the "wisdom" of modern spiritual science, or of the "living Christ." The books *Theosophy* and *How to Know Higher Worlds*, and also *Occult Science*, which had already been conceived in 1904, were, at least in part, Rosicrucian writings. Through his etheric body, Christian Rosenkreutz had furthered and supported them. ("Writings to which as little as possible was personally contributed," Rudolf Steiner wrote in 1914.[164]) In 1907, beginning with the Munich Congress, the aspect of "beauty" was implemented through the arts. Not long after Neuchâtel the same endeavor led to the birth of the first section of the "foundation."

Rudolf Steiner said little about the foundation and the "new way of working." No special "honors" would be bestowed on the foundation's twelve "curators." They would not be "dignitaries," but simply take on duties. In true Rosicrucian tradition, "everything personal" was to be excluded.[165] Rudolf Steiner said, "A very small group has formed that will have the task of separating the foundation from my own person and of establishing its independence."[166] Since the foundation was under the "direct protection" of Christian Rosenkreutz, Steiner's words probably described the attempt to connect a small esoteric community directly with Christian Rosenkreutz (and consequently with Master Jesus). Until then, only Rudolf Steiner had worked in such proximity to the masters on the promotion of anthroposophy. Now a small group of people was, independently of Rudolf Steiner, put in charge of cultivating greater receptivity for essential will impulses from the spiritual world. They were to work for these impulses in a way that excluded "everything remotely personal, and as a service to the future."[167]

Because of a serious personal transgression among the curators, Rudolf Steiner dissolved the foundation after a very short time[168] and never attempted to bring it to life again. The only remaining effect was the publication of a spiritual-scientific calendar for the year 1912. It was published at Easter and included the Soul Calendar. ("In the first and only meeting [of the foundation] it was decided to publish the calendar" [Wiesberger].[169]) No author was mentioned when the calendar was published "in the year 1879 after the birth of the 'I,'" as it said on the cover, in direct reference to the Mystery of Golgotha, which marked the true beginning of a new time. On January 27, 1912, Rudolf Steiner said in a lecture:

> Western humanity has the task of recognizing history. And Rosicrucianism has the mission of developing an attitude that recognizes a particular focus in historical evolution.... The Akashic Chronicles reveal that the focal point of human evolution is April 3 in the year 33 [the moment when Christ Jesus died on Golgotha]. It is of particular importance for Rosicrucianism that the focal point of human evolution lies there.[170]

According to Rudolf Steiner, we prepare our souls most effectively for the meeting with the etheric Christ if we live meditatively through the yearly cycle.[171] The calendar was an essential Rosicrucian impulse in that it related to the events of Golgotha and furthered inner development. It continued the work carried out by Rosicrucians for centuries on the more subtle processes in nature and in the course of the year: "sacrifice" as "sacred natural science." The calendar and Soul Calendar constituted the

Calendar for the year 1912
(In the year 1879 after the birth of the "I")

metamorphosis of that work for use in modern times. It could offer support to "any person" in "any situation,"[172] and could enhance human inner development in preparation for the experience of the reappearance in the etheric of the Christ being.

*

Rudolf Steiner continued to work with great determination even after the foundation of the "Society for Theosophical Art and Way of Living" had failed. This failing meant that a second "call" from the spiritual world or from Christian Rosenkreutz (since the foundation of the Theosophical Society) had become alienated or remained without response. One and a half years after the publication of the calendar, and only a few weeks after the performance of the fourth and last mystery drama, the foundation stone was laid for the "Johannes" building in Dornach.

The very early Rosicrucian communities referred to themselves as "Johannine Christians,"[173] as an allusion to Lazarus-John. The name first suggested for the building in Dornach was, as Rudolf Steiner pointed out more than once, not his choice; nor was it related to the evangelist. It referred to Johannes Thomasius, a prominent character in Steiner's mystery dramas. "The friends of anthroposophy first called the Goetheanum the 'Johannes building' when they initiated its construction more than ten years ago. The name does not derive from St. John, the Evangelist. It was chosen (not by me, but by others) in allusion to one of the characters in my mystery dramas, Johannes Thomasius, since the building was originally designated to serve, next to the cultivation of anthroposophy, as a place where those mysteries could be performed."[174] "The sponsors of the building named it the 'Johannes building' after a character in my mystery plays: *Johannes* Thomasius."[175] There was in fact more to the name[176] because Johannes Thomasius, the central figure of the first drama or Rosicrucian mystery, had been given his name for a reason: the Dornach building was deeply rooted in Christianity

Johannes building, March 1914

and in Johannine Rosicrucianism.[177] Rudolf Steiner hoped that
it would contribute in a major way to the revelation of the
"intentions of the living Christ" to the whole of civilization.[178]

From the very beginning, Rudolf Steiner intended to establish, through and in this building, an independent "school for
spiritual science," inspired by the original *scientific impulse*
of a Michaelic Rosicrucianism.[179] "The idea of a School for
Spiritual Science is the necessary conclusion we need to draw
from the fact that our time has been deemed worthy of receiving
certain spiritual knowledge," was said in the newsletter of the
Johannesbauverein (Johannes Building Association) of October
1911.[180] Besides the arts, it was obviously the scientific impulse
that was important to Christian Rosenkreutz. That impulse had
to be successful so that the esoteric movement could "be led into
the future" and spirituality implemented "in deed form" in the
various fields of life.

According to the notes Rudolf Steiner made in autumn 1907
for Edouard Schuré in the Documents de Barr, it was the aim of
the Rosicrucians to gradually disseminate esoteric wisdom *after*
the beginning of the Michael Age. As a "strictly secret school,"
they prepared "what was to be the public task of esotericism
around the turn of the twentieth century, once the exoteric natural
sciences had found the preliminary solution to certain problems."
Rudolf Steiner explained in several lectures that the Rosicrucians'
preparation consisted, among other things, in bringing about the
transformation of traditional ancient mystery wisdom, which
Christian Rosenkreutz had united and permeated with the Christ
impulse in a unique way (from East and West), so that the "archetypal wisdom of the world" could face the challenges of the scientific age. On June 3, 1909, Steiner said in Budapest:

> As it was, the great individuality of Christian Rosenkreutz
> foresaw the intellectual demands that would be posed by
> rationally thinking people. He knew that it was necessary
> at that time to pour all spiritual knowledge into a form that

would meet the requirements of the present times. We have to be clear about the fact that the task of the Rosicrucians was much more difficult than that of any other similar movement before, because their initial activities in the thir- teenth and fourteenth centuries coincided with the rapidly approaching materialism. All modern inventions, such as the steam engine, telegraph, and so on, had to place humanity firmly onto the physical plane. The Rosicrucians had to work for an age that has to think mathematically. They had to prepare for that; and as a result, they were often misunderstood.[181]

According to Steiner, the decision was made in the thirteenth or fourteenth century that the mystery knowledge guarded by the Rosicrucians was to become public knowledge in the forth- coming Michael Age. That knowledge was to leave the protection of the esoteric school to be absorbed by the prevailing culture. Esoteric wisdom would no longer be exclusive to small, esoteri- cally-minded groups, but potentially available to all people who chose it out of freedom.

Christian Rosenkreutz was the one who could clearly say that with the mysteries we have received the precious wisdom of the higher worlds. If we are satisfied with that, we can continue to do what was done so far: we can send out teachers who have gained their knowledge in our schools as soon as they have learned and understood the mysteries of archetypal cosmic wisdom. The ancient method of disseminating archetypal cosmic wisdom needs to be con- tinued. But something new is needed, too. He was able to say that many more people will want to find access to arche- typal cosmic wisdom. We can present it in the form avail- able to us today, but that requires a high degree of faith and the recognition of our authority. Humanity will lose that faith increasingly. The more people's capacity for judgment will grow, the less will they believe in their teachers as they did formerly. Faith and trust were necessary requirements for the earlier forms of communication. Now one has to say that in the future, people will want to see evidence of what they are told. They will say, "We want to apply the same logical thinking that we use when we observe the sensory world to what you tell us. More than rational thinking might be necessary to investigate the spiritual world, but we nevertheless want to examine it rationally." It was therefore necessary at the beginning of our era to pour the archetypal wisdom of the world into new forms. That was the task of the Rosicrucians: to transform archetypal cosmic wisdom gradually into a form that would suit the modern mind and soul.[182]

That is without doubt the intention of Rudolf Steiner's lectures and writings from the beginning of the twentieth century. "Anthroposophy is a path of inner development that strives to lead the human spirit to the cosmic spirit"[183]—in all who want that, and are ready for the "probation." As a modern spiritual science, anthroposophy "must prove itself to the sciences, to the *zeitgeist*; it must, and can, stand up to them."[184]

*

For that to happen, certain spiritual preparations were necessary. As Rudolf Steiner explained for the first time in Neuchâtel on December 18, 1912 (and shortly after in more detail in Berlin and Stuttgart), fundamental changes in the human spiritual constitution were connected with the "adaptation of the archetypal cosmic wisdom to the modern mind and soul" and to the development of intellectual materialism. The Rosicrucian goal of the dawning Michael Age could not be attained merely by adapting esoteric knowledge to modern scientific conceptual thinking. The human soul and the conditions of its incarnation had to be transformed.

The Rosicrucians saw the need to sacrifice their star wisdom temporarily in the second half of the fifteenth century.[185] When they began to enter deeply into the modern, increasingly materialistic sciences[186] in the sixteenth century, they realized that those sciences had the potential to obliterate all human spirituality.[187] Human development, as it was, aimed to rationalize all mental activity radically, and threatened to render access to the spiritual world through thinking increasingly impossible. According to Steiner, that course would be driven further in the nineteenth century through Michael's fight with the Ahrimanic powers. Michael would then attempt to assert himself in the etheric realm, to "clear the spiritual horizon" and prepare the reappearance of the Christ. As a result, the human intellect; human scientific, materialist thinking, would experience even more vehement attacks on earth than it had in the sixteenth century.

Rudolf Steiner explained that Christian Rosenkreutz knew of the coming developments in the history of consciousness, and convened an occult "conference" of leading Rosicrucians at the end of the sixteenth century. Among them were all the individualities who had taken on the education of Christian Rosenkreutz in the mid-thirteenth century, as well as other prominent spirits who supported the work of the community, either while they were incarnated on earth or from the spiritual world. "The conference was attended not only by individualities who were incarnated on earth at the time, but also by others who dwelt in spiritual worlds. Among those present was the individuality who had incarnated as Gautama Buddha in the sixth century before Christ."[188]

In this context, Rudolf Steiner referred to Gautama Buddha as the individuality who for a long time[189] was the "most intimate pupil and friend" of Christian Rosenkreutz.[190] He had united with the Luke Jesus child at the "turning point of time," and then he remained close to the Rosicrucian movement, which he actively helped to establish from the spiritual world.[191] At the occult conference of the late sixteenth century, which consisted of two meetings, Christian Rosenkreutz described the potential great danger to humanity. According to Rudolf Steiner, Christian Rosenkreutz spoke of the gradual emergence of two "classes" of people: a spiritually-minded minority, who would remain sensitive to the existence and activities of the spiritual world (and distant from the evolution of civilization), and a majority whose scientific thinking and soul-life would be increasingly informed by materialistic ideas. This situation would invariably lead to the "death of the soul." According to Rosenkreutz, the latter group would forfeit any possibility of rising up to the spiritual world in the future if they were to continue in the same way. It was therefore urgently necessary to introduce a counterbalance to the maya of scientific conceptual thinking. Christian Rosenkreutz said in this context that:

> Help could come only from an education that would not take place between birth and death, but between death and a new birth.[192]

In order to survive spiritually, human souls coming down to earthly incarnation at the end of the sixteenth century needed to receive different inner powers from cosmic spheres. In his writings and lectures, Rudolf Steiner, referred often and in great depth to the soul's journey from death to a new birth through the sphere of "unbornness."[193] He described in detail the powers and impulses absorbed by the soul in the planetary spheres after death and before birth; in spheres that underwent their own historical evolution. ("Yes, these cosmic bodies also evolve. Like the Earth, they undergo an evolution of descending and ascending. Each time we enter one of these cosmic bodies [Mars, Venus, or Mercury] after death, we find different circumstances there, and we take different experiences and impulses back with us into a new existence. Because other cosmic bodies also evolve, we bring different soul forces with us each time.")[194] In his presentations on Christian Rosenkreutz and the history of consciousness, which he started in Neuchâtel on December 18,

1912, Steiner emphasized the fatal impact that the Mars influences have had since the beginning of modern times. Rosenkreutz himself reported at the occult conference how the influence of Mars was originally good and supportive of humanity, but that now, because of a more "decadent" turn taken by the evolution of the planetary sphere, human souls grow ever more one-sided and materialistic. ("The Mars culture that human souls pass through between death and a new birth underwent a major crisis on Earth during the fifteenth and sixteenth centuries. At that time a development took place on Mars that was as catastrophic and incisive as the Mystery of Golgotha was on Earth.")[195] The effect of that development on Mars made it impossible for unborn souls to acquire powers to raise themselves above earthly matter, leading them to become devoted to matter instead. "Modern science arose from the decay of Mars."[196] A counter-impulse was needed in that sphere "because the salvation of the Earth depended on the Mars culture."[197] Rosenkreutz united the "salvation of the Earth" with the newly-to-be-acquired capacity of the human soul to retain its spirituality in the emerging scientific age through the ability to spiritualize the views and concepts gained through materialistic science.

> Humanity had to become proficient in scientific thinking. People had to learn to look at the world scientifically, and to develop ideas and concepts of the world that corresponded to the patterns of modern scientific thought. At the same time they needed to learn how to spiritualize the ideas, so that it would be possible to rise from the scientific view to spiritual heights. This possibility needed to be created.[198]

During the occult conference, Buddha made the decision to act as Christian Rosenkreutz' "messenger," and to help to induce the necessary transformation of the Mars sphere. At the suggestion of his friend Christian Rosenkreutz, he supported Christian evolution from the spiritual world.[199] *"In 1604, the individuality of Gautama Buddha did for Mars what the Mystery of Golgotha had done for the Earth."*[200] Rudolf Steiner spoke of the "cosmic sacrifice" of Buddha, who entered the aggressive sphere of Mars voluntarily to bring about its transformation, so that the human soul could be saved.

> The Mystery of Golgotha on Mars was different from that on the Earth; it was less overwhelming, less incisive, and it did not end in death. But you will get an idea of its significance if you consider that the most sublime prince of peace and love, the bearer of compassion on Earth, was sent to Mars as the leader of the entire Mars evolution.[201]

> Just as the substance of the Christ flowed from the Mystery of Golgotha, the peace substance of Buddha streamed onto the Mars sphere, where it has been active ever since.[202]

Since Buddha began his cosmic-planetary work in 1604, which was twice seven years before the beginning of the Thirty Years' War—and at the time of the *Chymical Wedding*; the opening of Rosenkreutz' tomb (*Fama*); the most dramatic scientific, social, and religious upheavals in Central Europe; and a particular astronomical constellation[203]—different forces have entered the human soul on its cosmic journey through the sphere of Mars between death and a new birth. They are forces that allow us to free ourselves from the compulsions of earthly conditions, and to deepen our inner life and become free and independent in our thinking, however strongly external conditions tend toward uniformity and collectivism.[204] According to Rudolf Steiner, the powers that Christian Rosenkreutz helped to prepare cosmically in the early seventeenth century have since been active in the earthly organization of free human individuality and in modern spirituality. To those powers we owe the ability to lead a "healthy esoteric everyday life," which is essential, as Rudolf

Steiner tended to emphasize in his early reflections on inner development. Since the beginning of the modern era, we are able to meditate in the midst of our material life, without having to withdraw from it, and we can at any time return to our ordinary tasks.

> When modern spiritual students meditate in the way indicated by Christian Rosenkreutz, forces stream to the Earth, sent by Buddha who is the redeemer of Mars.[205]

All these processes were preparations for the Michael Age, which started at the end of the nineteenth century, and which would not have been possible without them. The scientific impulse arising from Rudolf Steiner's independent "School for Spiritual Science" (the purpose of the Johannes building) was connected with those preparations. At Rudolf Steiner's wish, the building was given the name "Goetheanum" in late autumn 1917, following a lecture on the scientific foundations of anthroposophy in Basel on October 18, 1917. There he said, "I would like to name the anthroposophic view of the world, which arises from scientific research in the way characterized by me, after the sources ... that originally inspired it in me. I would like to call this view of the world 'Goetheanism'; and the ... building over in Dornach that is dedicated to it, I would call the 'Goetheanum.'"[206] Rudolf Steiner's path to anthroposophy was guided by Christian Rosenkreutz and Master Jesus. It included Goethe and his natural-scientific views, which were a "possible starting point for ascending to spiritual heights" in accordance with what Christian Rosenkreutz had prepared spiritually in the seventeenth century. As "Goetheanum," the "Johannes building" was to serve that scientific endeavor. The "School for Spiritual Science" was to carry the newly found mystery wisdom into all areas of life, to the "modern mind and soul," as a *free* force in our present civilization, independent of current opinions and prevailing paradigms.

Johannes building, April 1915

*

In January 1916, a year and a half before the Goetheanum received its name, publisher and alchemist Baron Alexander von Bernus, who was well disposed toward anthroposophy, asked Rudolf Steiner to write the introduction to a new edition of the *Chymical Wedding of Christian Rosenkreutz, Anno 1459.* Both the introduction and the *Chymical Wedding* were to be printed in the cultural magazine published by von Bernus, *Das Reich.*[207] ("If you would kindly consider writing even a very brief introduction to this new edition, it would be highly significant.") Steiner valued von Bernus and his commitment, and offered his essay "Knowledge of the Condition between Death and a New Birth" as a contribution to the first issue of *Das Reich,* which included the first part of the *Chymical Wedding.* Pleased about von Bernus' initiative, Steiner also agreed to write the introduction. Intimate ties connect the appearance of the first Rosicrucian writings in the early seventeenth century, the essay "Knowledge of the Condition between Death and a New Birth," the cosmic events of 1604, and the intention to establish the independent School for Spiritual Science in Dornach. Interestingly, Ferdinand Maack, the Berlin publisher of the previous German edition of the *Chymical Wedding* (1913), had written disparagingly in 1912 about the Dornach foundation (the "Theosophical university for spiritual science"), referring to Rudolf Steiner as having been "brought up by Jesuits."[208] Annie Besant reiterated the accusation shortly afterward. ("The German General Secretary, educated by the Jesuits...."[209]) The adversarial powers gathered, or were even fully engaged, in an attempt to "eradicate the Christ principle"[210] from Western culture, as Rudolf Steiner wrote in Barr in 1907.

It took Rudolf Steiner some time to compose his introduction to the *Chymical Wedding.* When he sent von Bernus the first part of his introduction in September 1917, he explained in the cover letter:

DIE CHYMISCHE HOCHZEIT DES CHRISTIAN ROSENKREUTZ

RUDOLF STEINER

I.

Wer das Wesen der Erlebnisse kennt, welche die Menschenseele macht, wenn sie sich die Eingangspforten zur geistigen Welt eröffnet hat, der braucht nur wenige Seiten der „Chymischen Hochzeit Christiani Rosencreutz anno 1459" zu lesen, um zu erkennen, daß die Darstellung des Buches sich auf wirkliche geistige Erfahrungen bezieht. Subjektiv ersonnene Bilder verraten sich als solche demjenigen, der Einsicht in die geistige Wirklichkeit hat, weil sie weder in ihrer eigenen Gestalt, noch in der Art, wie sie aneinandergereiht werden, dieser Wirklichkeit vollkommen entsprechen können. — Damit scheint der Gesichtspunkt gegeben, von dem aus die „Chymische Hochzeit" zunächst betrachtet werden kann. Man kann den geschilderten Erlebnissen gewissermaßen seelisch nachgehen und erforschen, was die Einsicht in geistige Wirklichkeiten zu ihnen zu sagen hat. Unbekümmert um alles, was über dieses Buch geschrieben worden ist, soll der damit gekennzeichnete Gesichtspunkt hier zunächst eingenommen werden. Aus dem Buche selbst soll geholt werden, was es sagen will. Dann erst kann über Fragen gesprochen werden, welche viele Betrachter stellen, bevor dafür eine genügende Grundlage geschaffen ist.
In sieben seelische Tagewerke sind die Erlebnisse des Wanderers zur „chymischen Hochzeit" gegliedert. Der erste Tag beginnt damit, daß dem Träger der Erlebnisse Imaginationen vor die Seele treten, die seinen Entschluß reifen lassen, die Wanderung zu beginnen. Die Schilderung ist so gehalten, daß sie besondere Sorgfalt des Darstellers erkennen läßt, zu unterschieden zwischen dem, was der Träger der Erlebnisse zur Zeit, da er ein „Gesicht" hat, von demselben versteht, und dem, was seiner Einsicht noch verborgen ist. Ebenso ist unterschieden, was aus der geistigen Welt an den Schauenden herantritt, ohne daß sein Wille daran beteiligt ist, und was durch diesen Willen herbeigeführt wird. Das erste Erlebnis ist kein willkürlich herbeigeführtes und nicht ein solches, das der Schauende völlig versteht. Es bringt ihm die Möglichkeit, in die geistige Welt einzutreten. Es

393

From Rudolf Steiner's article on the *Chymical Wedding*

I had to phrase certain facts in the essay very carefully to allow for their publication. There are occultists who hold that matters such as references to deception, aging (death), and consciousness must not be published. But their view has been overtaken by occult insights better suited to *our time*. I had to find a way of expressing myself that was right for publication. It is now the time for saying such things.[211] [author emphasis]

Von Bernus must have been surprised at these words, since Rudolf Steiner, in the preceding one and a half years, had published much heftier occult matters than "references to deception, aging (death), and consciousness." Direct references to Christian Rosenkreutz and his stream, however, called for particular caution, especially in times of conflict and violence.[212]

When Steiner sent in the third part, six months later, he wrote:

In the essay, I have been as explicit as one can be at present in interpreting the *Chymical Wedding*. I would go further only if someone claimed that the spirit of my interpretation was wrong. In the given context, exoteric Rosicrucian literature certainly does not need to be given more consideration than I have given it at the end of the essay. What I have written at the very end about Andreae's view of Rosicrucianism is the outcome of real spiritual-scientific research. *That* will provoke skepticism among those who have written about the matter so far. But my spiritual-scientific findings are well founded. Should I see myself coerced into describing their origin in more detail (in case of objections), that would exceed the margins of an essay about the *Chymical Wedding*. For now, I think that what I have written will suffice.[213] [author's emphasis]

Rudolf Steiner saw the content of the *Chymical Wedding* as authentic and spiritually true, despite the objections that might be raised against its author, the Swabian theologian Johann Valentin Andreae (1586-1654). Rudolf Steiner wrote at the beginning of the essay, "Those who are familiar with what the human soul experiences, once it has found access to the spiritual world, need only to read a few pages of the *Chymical Wedding Christiani Rosenkreutz Anno 1459* to know that the descriptions they find there relate to genuine spiritual experiences." He ended with the words:

> [these considerations] corroborate the view that the work published by Andreae indicates the direction one needs to pursue in order to find out about the true quality of higher knowledge. These considerations seek to confirm that the *Chymical Wedding* describes the special quality of spiritual knowledge that has been required since the fifteenth century. To those who agree with the author of these considerations about the content of the *Chymical Wedding*, it will hold *a historical message from a spiritual stream in Europe that reaches back to the fifteenth century*, and that has as its goal the attainment of knowledge about what lies behind the external phenomena of the world.[214] [author emphasis]

According to Steiner, Andreae composed the *Chymical Wedding* as a very young man, out of intuition; it was his work, but it was not born from his spirit. "As a young man he was granted by this spiritual stream the disposition to present images of that stream *without the interference of his own thinking*."[215] Andreae went on to philosophize in an unfortunate way about his own early writings, which he had not understood when he was writing them down.[216] In a lecture to members of the Anthroposophical Society, Rudolf Steiner explained in summer 1918: "... A wholly different power spoke through him [while he was writing].... His hand wrote it down; his body was present, but another spiritual power spoke through him. The spiritual power, who was not

Chymische Hoch
zeit:
Chriſtiani Roſencreütz
ANNO 1459.

Arcana publicata vileſcunt; & gratiam prophanata amittunt.

Ergo: ne Margaritas obijce porcis, ſeu Aſino ſubſterne roſas.

Straßburg/
In Verlägung / Lazari Zetzners.

Anno M. DC. aVI.

Chymical Wedding: *Christiani Rosenkreutz Anno 1459,*
first edition, Strasbourg, 1616

incarnated on earth at the time, sought to make these contents known to humanity in the way they were written down."[217] *"It is a work that is inspired through and through,"* Steiner said about the *Chymical Wedding* in the Karma Lectures of 1924.[218] He did not name the "spiritual power, who was not incarnated on earth at the time"—the power that inspired Andreae at the beginning of the seventeenth century and that spoke through the *Chymical Wedding.* ("Again and again I was driven by an elusive spirit" [Andreae].[219]) Much of what Steiner said in the context, however, seems to indicate that it was Christian Rosenkreutz himself.

*

The contents of the *Chymical Wedding* and other Rosicrucian writings disseminated in the first two decades of the seventeenth century constituted a "historical message from a spiritual stream in Europe that reaches back to the fifteenth century," as Rudolf Steiner wrote in *Das Reich.* He did not further elaborate on the spiritual origin of the Rosicrucians in his introductory articles, but provided meticulous, detailed comments on the imagery of the *Chymical Wedding* from the point of view of anthroposophy.[220] In private lectures to members of the Anthroposophical Society, he acknowledged for the first time the fundamental significance of the Rosicrucian writings that first appeared in the early seventeenth century. Previously, Rudolf Steiner had tended to understate their importance for gaining insight into the origin of the Rosicrucian movement. Now he presented them as part of an important social impulse of their time. "...there was indeed a striving to introduce a social structure that corresponded to the true human essence. This is how the *Chymical Wedding of Christian Rosenkreutz* came to be written by one 'Valentin Andreae,' who also wrote a book about the *Universal Reformation of the Entire World*, in which he gave a broad sketch of the political situation and the way social conditions

ought to develop. The Thirty Years' War swept all that away"
(August 26, 1918).[221]

All three of Andreae's writings, which "at first glance seem
to be satires," carried the important impulse for a "deepening
of the spiritual insight into nature to the point…*where a more
profound understanding of the laws of nature can lead to the
discovery of the laws of social coexistence, where the laws
of human social life can be found*," as Rudolf Steiner said in
Dornach in October 1917,[222] a few days before he proposed to
name the building in Dornach after Goethe. Such a deepened
understanding was exactly what Goethe, who was "profoundly
initiated in the Rosicrucian mysteries,"[223] had in mind[224] when
he wrote his *Tale of the Green Snake and the Beautiful Lily* (as
an "alchemistic initiation in the form established by Christian
Rosenkreutz"[225]).

According to Rudolf Steiner, the *Chymical Wedding* provides
occult images of real nature processes. Its central impulse, which
goes back to Christian Rosenkreutz, is to gain knowledge of
social laws through a deepened spiritual understanding of nature,
at a time that is historically critical. "Then the Thirty Years'
War came, burying much of what should have been brought
to humanity. At the time of the Thirty Years' War, humanity
was meant to understand matters that failed to be understood,
because they were buried. The *Chymical Wedding* was written
by the individual who called himself Johann Valentin Andreae.
It is a proven fact that it was written by 1603. It remained unno-
ticed because the Thirty Years' War broke out in 1618. Such
things happen sometimes before the outbreak of wars."[226] The
Rosicrucian writings found an immense response; but they also
provoked resistance, and even hatred, persecution, and the will
to destroy, from the Jesuits, among others."[227] As a result the
brotherhood kept in the background, giving up its initial intention to work openly.

When Rudolf Steiner spoke in 1917/18 about the Rosicrucian
social impulse of the early seventeenth century, he looked back

on an extended period of important spiritual research that was
also connected with the deepening "of the spiritual insight into
nature" to the point where "a more profound understanding
of the laws of nature can lead to the discovery of the laws
of social coexistence, where the laws of human social life can
be found." On March 15, 1917, Steiner began to present his
ideas of the functional threefoldness of the human organism
in Berlin.[228] In May 1917, he expounded the threefoldness of
the social organism to Count Otto Lerchenfeld[229] as the basis
for a new, peaceful order in Europe that would put an end to
war and bring about the renewal of international and domestic
relations.[230] Rudolf Steiner had researched both concepts of
threefoldness thoroughly in decades of spiritual investigation.
They were immensely important for the future of humanity.
The final breakthrough of his Michaelic vision[230a] had taken
place in the middle of World War I. At the same time, Steiner
had again immersed himself deeply into the Rosicrucian writings of the early seventeenth century. It seems likely that it
was not until then that Rudolf Steiner became fully aware
of the immense social significance of those writings, and of
the Rosicrucian impulse underlying them, and that the breakthrough in his own research received "strength and support"
from that same source.

When speaking about Johann Valentin Andreae's early seventeenth century writings, Rudolf Steiner said in Berlin on September
1917:

> Johann Valentin Andreae had a great spiritual movement
> in mind. His thoughts and feelings arose from a long period
> of preparation. Two things were important at the time:
> what Valentin Andreae wanted and what led to the Thirty
> Years' War, which started in 1618 and lasted until 1648.
> What led to the Thirty Years' War rendered the movement
> impossible that Johann Valentin Andreae had intended
> to initiate. Much could be said if one wanted to specify

VON SEELENRÄTSELN

I. ANTHROPOLOGIE UND ANTHROPOSOPHIE

II. MAX DESSOIR ÜBER ANTHROPOSOPHIE

III. FRANZ BRENTANO (EIN NACHRUF).

VON

RUDOLF STEINER.

1.—4. TAUSEND.

1917.

PHILOSOPHISCH-ANTHROPOSOPHISCHER VERLAG
(BERLIN W, MOTZSTRASSE 17).

Original edition of Steiner's *Riddles of the Soul*, 1917.
First written account of physiological threefoldness

the reasons why he failed. Some attempts are undertaken
and fail, but later they are successful. There was a way of
moving forward at the time. Today it is again necessary to
stand within two streams that need to interact with one
another: on the one hand, the intentions of anthroposophy
that arise from the impulses of human evolution; and on
the other, what has led to events that resemble those of the
Thirty Years' War. It will be the task of humanity not to
undo again what needs to be done.[231]

In 1917 a new important attempt was undertaken from the spiritual world (or aided *by* the spiritual world) to "ensure that a social
structure was introduced that would correspond to the true human
essence": the spiritual impulse of the threefold social organism,
which corresponds wholly to the true essence of humanity. Christian
Rosenkreutz inspired Johann Valentin Andreae, who did not know
what he was writing, and supported Rudolf Steiner, who worked in
his interest out of initiated consciousness.

Paul Regenstreif called attention to the fact that not only the
unresolved state of affairs at the end of World War I but also
Rudolf Steiner's ideas and activities in the years before the war
were very similar to the situation before the outbreak of the
Thirty Years' War. "In 1614 the *Fama Fraternitatis* appeared; in
1615 the *Confessio*; in 1616 the *Chymical Wedding of Christian
Rosenkreutz*, which that had been written as early as 1603. In
1618 the Thirty Years' War came with the *Confessio*,[232] and
swept away the noble intentions of the *Fama Fraternitatis*."
Based on that statement by Rudolf Steiner, Regenstreif drew the
following parallel: "In 1910, Steiner announced the appearance
of the etheric Christ and delivered his lectures on the "Mission
of the Folk Souls." In 1911 he spoke about the Matreya Buddha
and Christian Rosenkreutz, and in 1912/13 he disclosed to
humanity the beginning of the Fifth Gospel."[233]

*

On June 9, 1918, a few months before the end of World
War I, Rudolf Steiner visited Count Ludwig Polzer Hoditz,
a staunch advocate of the threefold social order at Austria's
imperial court. Steiner performed a ritual act "under the sign of
the Rosy Cross" at Hoditz' castle, Tannbach.[234] There he also
emphasized that at the beginning of the seventeenth century the
people of Central Europe would have been receptive to a spiritual impulse, but that the Thirty Years' War and the powers and
forces behind it had prevented the impulse from unfolding in
a larger group of people.[235] From Tannstein, Steiner traveled
on to Prague and to Castle Karlstein, which, under Charles IV,
had been the European spiritual center around the middle of
the fourteenth century.[236] On his return to Berlin, Steiner spoke
about his visit to Karlstein and his walk up to the Chapel of the
Holy Cross:

> You find some quite primitive paintings in the stairwell;
> but what is depicted there throughout the whole staircase,
> in however primitive a manner? The Chymical Wedding of
> Christian Rosenkreutz! You walk through this 'Chemical
> Wedding' that leads you to a Grail chapel. Then the Thirty
> Years' War came, after the *Chymical Wedding* had been
> written, but the waves of the Thirty Years buried its signifi-
> cance. *Lessons must be drawn from that, for it must not
> happen a second time.*[237] [author's emphasis]

Although Rudolf Steiner did all he could to support the
Christian direction of human evolution in the years that
followed, the threefold social order was indeed prevented from
taking effect by the adversarial powers. A greater urgency is
evident in Steiner's life and work after World War I than ever
before.[238] Nothing was to be left untried in the effort to introduce future impulses into the difficult and critical situation.
In 1919, Rudolf Steiner published his "Appeal to the German
People and the Cultural World"; and three essays on the social

Wall paintings in the staircase of Castle Karlstein,
leading up to the Chapel of the Holy Cross

question and social threefoldness were printed in the April issue
of von Bernus' magazine *Das Reich*, three years after it had
featured the first part of the *Chymical Wedding*. Resistance was
massive—as massive as at the time of the Thirty Years' War.
Nazi Fascism, which would bring destruction to Central Europe and
the whole world, began to raise its head: the "figures of anti-
Christianity"[239] that Steiner clearly recognized and described.
"People are preparing for the next great world war. Culture will
be further destroyed."[240] "There is a strong obsession in people
with the powers of evil, with the love for evil."[241] Threefoldness
failed. But Steiner continued to work untiringly.

If Rosicrucianism's "highest endeavor" was, and still is, "to
unveil the Christ intentions in wisdom, beauty, and deed," we
can say that the last stage of Rudolf Steiner's work, which began
during World War I, represented the third aspect, the "deed"
aspect of his Christian-Rosicrucian activities. The impulses
of resurrection that Rudolf Steiner introduced into the social
sphere, and also into medicine, education, and agriculture,
revealed the Christ intentions of the present and the future:
they were the Christian-Michaelic expression of what urgently
needed to be realized, or at the very least prepared. (*"Doing
anthroposophy!"*[242]) Again, Christian Rosenkreutz, "the great
servant of Christ Jesus," was the spiritual influence behind all
these efforts. "Christian Rosenkreutz always stands as inspiration close to those he has chosen."[243]

Only a few of those who worked by Rudolf Steiner's side
were fully aware of those efforts and able "to understand
that the development of the anthroposophic cause is a task
of the present civilization."[244] Rudolf Steiner's efforts were
surrounded by powerful opponents, who strove to elimi-
nate him and his work; at the end of 1922, they succeeded
in totally destroying by arson his school for spiritual science
in Dornach, the Goetheanum. The fire started in the "White
Room," the place where three months earlier the first "Act
of Consecration" had been celebrated, supported by Rudolf

Goetheanum ruin after the fire

Steiner and the powers who guided him, among whom Master Jesus was the foremost.

*

Seven years after presenting the idea of the threefold human and social order—and twice seven years after the performance of the first mystery drama as a "Rosicrucian mystery"[245]—Rudolf Steiner re-founded the Anthroposophical Society in a solemn, powerful act, after years of social crises and stagnation.[246]

A "new impulse" had to come, as he said during the Christmas Conference of the Anthroposophical Society 1923/24, which would take hold of and penetrate the School for Spiritual Science and the Society in Dornach to enable them to fulfill their task in the face of the adversities of the time:

> What has to radiate out now from Dornach needs to receive impetus from an impulse that does not come from the earth, but from the spiritual world. Here, we want to generate the strength to pursue the impulses from the spiritual world.[247]

> The spiritual world has certain intentions regarding humanity at this particular time of human evolution. It wants to bring that intention to practical realization in the most varied fields of life, and it is up to us to follow, clearly and truly, the impulses that come from the spiritual world.[248]

At that crucial moment in history ("much that is of tremendous impact is being decided at this moment for humanity"[249]), the center at Dornach, and with it the whole Anthroposophical Society, had to "penetrate the full seriousness of esotericism"[250] and become active in the world out of that esoteric impulse. "It needs a stronger impact now than previously for the spirit that humanity needs to enter."[251]

During the spiritual "conference" at the turn of the seventeenth century, Christian Rosenkreutz had warned that a great number of people would experience a real "death of soul" because of the materialism by which they were increasingly dominated, and they would forfeit the possibility of finding access to the spiritual world. Rosenkreutz had prepared the necessary conditions for a countermovement, which was to be implemented in practice in the twentieth century through the School for Spiritual Science in Dornach. Despite the preparations undertaken by Rosenkreutz and the powers close to him, even decades after the age of Michael had begun, the situation remained utterly critical. Rudolf Steiner explained on January 1, 1924, that because of the continuing predominance of materialism human souls were excluded from entering the spiritual world in the night-sphere of their existence, that they were rejected by the Guardian of the Threshold. If these conditions continued to prevail, there would be catastrophic consequences that would fatally affect even human incarnations:

> If the situation experienced before the Guardian of the Threshold were to continue, and if humanity were exposed for long enough to the traditional knowledge acquired in schools today, sleep would become life. Human souls would pass through the gates of death into the spiritual world, but they would be unable to carry the power of ideas into their next earthly life. With today's thinking we can enter, but not leave, the spiritual world. We would leave the spiritual world with paralyzed souls.
>
> You see, present civilization can be founded on the kind of spiritual life that has been cultivated for such a long time, but life cannot be founded on it. Present civilization could continue as it is for some time. Human souls would know nothing of the Guardian of the Threshold when they are awake, and the Guardian would reject them in their sleep to save them from becoming paralyzed. As a

result, future humanity would be born without rationality; without the possibility of putting ideas into practice. Thinking and living ideas would disappear from the earth. The earth would be populated by a sick human species that would be guided only by instincts: evil feelings and emotions alone would govern human evolution, unguided by the power of ideas.[252]

During his lifetime, Rudolf Steiner did much to counteract this tendency with his spiritual-scientific writings and lectures and his esoteric school, and also by creating institutions for a "free" or "liberated" spiritual life. The Goetheanum in particular, the Dornach School for Spiritual Science, as a Rosicrucian Johannine building, had a special mission in the Michael Age. Yet, because of the paralysis of the Anthroposophical Society and the hostile circumstances at the time, it made little progress. In 1923/24 Rudolf Steiner undertook a last determined effort to steer the movement into the future:

Here in Dornach must be the place where important direct experiences of the spiritual world can be described to people who wish to hear about them. Here, we must find the strength to go beyond vague indications of a possible spiritual world, as it is done in today's theoretical, dialectic-empirical sciences. If Dornach wants to fulfill its mission, people must be able to hear openly here about the impulses from the spiritual world that enter into natural existence and infuse nature. People must be able to hear in Dornach about real spiritual experiences, powers, and entities. This must be the school for true spiritual science. In the future, we must not shrink back from the challenges of today's science that leads us, as I described, before the Guardian of the Threshold in a state of sleep. It must be possible for people to gain, in Dornach, the strength to meet the spiritual world face-to-face, spiritually speaking, and to learn from the spiritual world.... In Dornach we will create a center of spiritual knowledge.[253]

At the Christmas Conference 1923/24, when Rudolf Steiner re-founded the General Anthroposophical Society, through a further initiate's impulse, he included as its "heart and soul" the "esoteric school of the Goetheanum." The esoteric "Michael School"[254] was to grow into a real mystery school that would be appropriate for the times, and be composed of three classes. Out of that school as a Christian mystery site, various departments or "sections" would work in the future, giving impulses from the "full seriousness of esotericism" to achieve what would still be possible to achieve in those critical times.[255] Rudolf Steiner referred to the esoteric executive council at the Goetheanum (the group around him) as an "initiative council." "It needs an initiative council that takes hold of the tasks that the spiritual world ascribes to the anthroposophic movement. It needs to take on those tasks and bring them into the world...."[256]

Twelve years earlier, at the end of 1911, following the important lectures about Christian Rosenkreutz in Neuchâtel, the attempt to found a "Society for Theosophical Art and Way of Living" and place it under the "direct protection" of Christian Rosenkreutz had failed because of human inadequacy. At the time, Steiner had also intended to establish an initiative body that would receive and work out of direct impulses from the spiritual world. Now he decided to undertake another, and final, attempt to achieve that.

Rudolf Steiner prepared his new effort to create an esoteric social community with a lecture course about the mysteries, concluding with a presentation of the medieval Rosicrucian mysteries that constituted the transition to modern times.[257] In his evening lectures at the Christmas Conference, Steiner spoke in great detail about the Rosicrucians, particularly about their knowledge of anthropology and medicine,[258] and that the School for Spiritual Science in Dornach was to have "a healing effect" on the civilization of the twentieth century and beyond.[259] After that conference, he gave two more lecture cycles: on the Medieval mystery sites, Rosicrucianism, and modern initiation[260] and on the esoteric and exoteric foundations of a new medicine inspired by Rosicrucianism and anthroposophy.[261] According to Rudolf Steiner, the Rosicrucian school founded in the thirteenth and fourteenth centuries was an "institution of spiritual research and spiritual knowledge" that worked therapeutically and had success-ful physicians who brought real mystery knowledge to their time through the way they practiced medicine. The "healing" impulse of the new Dornach school undoubtedly follows in that tradition and is part of the central Christ impulses of our times: "All education, all cultural influences must be health-giving. The healing aspect is the very essence of the Christ impulse."[262] At the Christmas Conference 1923/24, he referred to medicine[263] as the "most essen-tial practical application of human knowledge." He created the Foundation Stone Meditation around the three Rosicrucian mot-toes, which he spoke mantrically at the beginning of the Act of Consecration at Christmas:

> Ex Deo nascimur
> In Christo morimur
> Per Spiritum Sanctum reviviscimus.

> From God we are born
> In Christ death will turn to life
> In the spirit's cosmic thoughts the soul will awaken.[264]

The Foundation Stone itself, the culmination of the Christmas conference,[265] was not a philosophers' stone, a "stone of wisdom" —it was a stone of love.[266] "Wisdom is a prerequisite of love; love arises from wisdom when it is reborn in the 'I'" (Rudolf Steiner[267]).

The question arises if perhaps the last verse of the Foundation Stone Meditation is an appeal or call to the sphere of *Master Jesus* in the light of Michael, after the microcosmic and macrocosmic connections of the first three Rosicrucian verses and in the scope

In der Zeiten Wende
Trat das Welten-Geistes-Licht
In den irdischen Wesensstrom;
Nacht-Dunkel
Hatte ausgewaltet;
Taghelles Licht
Erstrahlte in Menschenseelen;
Licht,
Das erwärmet
Die armen Hirtenherzen;
Licht,
Das erleuchtet
Die weisen Königshäupter.

Göttliches Licht,
Christus-Sonne
Erwärme
Unsere Herzen;
Erleuchte
Unsere Häupter;

Dass gut werde,
Was wir
Aus Herzen gründen,
Was wir
Aus Häuptern führen,
Wollen.

Foundation Stone Meditation, 4th verse

of what resounds in the words *"I want to feel the Christ being"* from the esoteric lessons after the Christmas Conference.[268] The fourth verse of the Foundation Stone Meditation returns to the real incarnation of Christ at the turning point of time—to the mystery of the baptism at Jordan, the mystery of the incarnation of Christ Jesus.[269] The Solomon Jesus (the Zarathustra individuality) played an instrumental part in that mystery, and from the "deepest soul and heart forces," the knowledge and love of Christ turned toward the future, toward a new selfless community as the beginning of a new culture of the future:

> At the turning point of time
> The Spirit-Light of the world
> Entered the stream of earthly being.
> Darkness of night
> Had held its sway,
> Day-radiant light
> streamed into human souls.
> Light that gives warmth
> To simple shepherds' hearts.
> Light that enlightens
> The wise heads of kings.
>
> Light Divine
> Christ-Sun
> Warm our hearts,
> Enlighten our heads,
> That good may become
> What from our hearts we would found
> And from our heads direct
> With single purpose.[270]

There is little evidence that Rudolf Steiner's esoteric masters Christian Rosenkreutz and Master Jesus suggested to Rudolf Steiner that he should hold the Christmas Conference, or even how to hold it. It is more likely that he himself made the decision to give the Anthroposophical Society and the School for Spiritual Science a new spiritual foundation in those crisis times (seven weeks after Adolf Hitler's first attempted coup), that it was Steiner's decision to take on the leadership of the Anthroposophical Society himself in full responsibility and unite the whole esoteric movement with the ailing organism of the Society. Despite all the social failures he had experienced, Steiner took it upon himself to move forward spiritually, ready to bear all the consequences. He spoke repeatedly of the great "risk" involved in taking that step. The people closest to him were aware of that too, although they could not see what stood behind his deed. *"It was a tremendous risk and one could almost feel and sense the shaking of the entire cosmos when that step was taken,"* Ita Wegman wrote.[271]

The entire Christmas Conference was a true mystery ritual. Rudolf Steiner was no longer alone when he performed it. After having made the decision in freedom, he acted for and with his masters and Michael. He referred to the "esoteric school of the Goetheanum," which began its work in mid-February 1924, as a "Michael School." It was also intimately connected with Christian Rosenkreutz.[272] In the Christmas Conference, the joint impulse of Michael and Christian Rosenkreutz was reinforced in the heart of the Anthroposophical Society and brought to the awareness of its members worldwide, so that together they could go toward the future to face the challenges and crises of the twentieth century and beyond. "If we look out into the world today, we see (and have seen for years) extreme destructive potential. There are powers at work that enable us to sense the abyss that Western civilization is moving toward," Rudolf Steiner said in his concluding address of the conference.[273] Never before in his life and work had he used the term "destructive potential." But Michael fought against the "dragon"; and in 1910 Rudolf Steiner had said about the stream of Christian Rosenkreutz: *"Rosicrucianism carries impulses that will be used to oppose the demons.*"[274] Christian Rosenkreutz was initiated in 1459 by Mani, who knows about the secrets and the purpose of evil. Mani was concerned with the "true harmony of all religions" and the future transformation of evil, in preparation for another culture that is also actively supported by Master Jesus.

*

The physician Ita Wegman, in a life-changing meeting in 1907 in Munich, chose Rudolf Steiner and his esoteric school; that is, Christian Rosenkreutz and Master Jesus.[275] Wegman supported Rudolf Steiner *full of courage* in the realization of his Christmas Conference intentions. ("And on this Dornach hill/the soul must, full of courage, find itself, so it can learn that spirit sun does not cast shadows, but weaves the dawn's true light around the rose cross stars."[276]) In the fall of 1924, after Ita Wegman had undergone twelve months of special esoteric training[277] and a special esoteric ritual, Rudolf Steiner admitted her as co-leader to the First Class of the Michael School, handing over to her his rose cross. (Cf. p. 97ff). With Ita Wegman, who represented the healing aspect of the Christmas Conference impulse, and who stood close to Michael and the Rosicrucian stream (and who fought in the first ranks against the demons), Rudolf Steiner often spoke about Christian Rosenkreutz, the "great servant of Christ Jesus." Above her desk in the clinic, where she often saw patients together with Rudolf Steiner, she had (possibly on Steiner's advice) put up a precious copy of Hans Memling's St. John altarpiece from the great medieval hospital of a Johannine brotherhood in the Belgian town of Bruges. Steiner, who never referred in his lectures to the first places of activity of the early Rosicrucians, might well have passed on such information to Ita Wegman personally, referring her to the brotherhood of the St. John Hospital in Bruges, which was located directly opposite St. John's Church.

Ita Wegman was also Rudolf Steiner's physician, and she looked after him during the last six months of his life. Even

Ich halte die Sonne in mir
Sie führet als König mich in die Welt

Ich halte den Mond in mir
Sie meine Gestalt erhält

Ich halte Mercur in mir
Er Sonne und Mond zusammenhält

Ich halte Venus in mir
Ohne ihre Liebe ist alles nichts

Sie mit Mars sich vereinet
Der mein Wesen in Worte spricht

Daß Jupiter alles erleuchtet
mit weisem Licht

Und Saturn der reife
In mir erstrahlet meines Wesens Farben

Rudolf Steiner: meditation for Ita Wegman

Rosicrucian illustration from Ita Wegman's Estate

at that time, the powers opposed to him surrounded and attacked his life and work.[278] Rudolf Steiner prayed and meditated regularly with Ita Wegman; for the last time in the afternoon of March 29, 1925, the day before he died. *"Christian Rosenkreutz played a major part in these meditations"* (Ita Wegman).[279]

Ita Wegman wrote of Rudolf Steiner's death on the morning of March 30, 1925, in his Dornach studio, which formed part of the carpentry complex of the destroyed first Goetheanum:

> His passing away was like a miracle. He left quite naturally. It seemed to me as if the die was cast in the last moment. And once it was cast there was no struggle, no attempt to stay on earth. For a while his gaze remained steady and calm; then he said a few kind words to me, and deliberately he closed his eyes and folded his hands.[280]

> In my work as a physician I had never seen anyone pass away so quickly from the earth. The die had been cast and the other activity in the spiritual world began immediately. No further preparations were needed.[281]

✻

Rosicrucian illustration from Ita Wegman's estate

Rudolf Steiner (1861-1925)

Epilogue

Little is known about Rudolf Steiner's special relationship with Christian Rosenkreutz. Steiner spoke only very rarely about the spiritual dimension of his encounter with Rosenkreutz, and only to the very few of his coworkers whom he fully trusted. In 1911 he said in Neuchâtel that Christian Rosenkreutz was in incarnation, mentioning physical encounters with him in conversation with some people.[282] The most essential aspect of that relationship was without doubt its spiritual dimension.

Rudolf Steiner worked on behalf of Christian Rosenkreutz, who was to "lead the esoteric movement into the future." Up to 1914, he would let Christian Rosenkreutz' own words resound in some of the lessons of his esoteric school: "The future lives in us as the rosy dawn. Consider that, and take in what the Master Christian Rosenkreutz speaks to you."[283] Elisabeth Vreede described how, in the esoteric lessons, Steiner was able to speak out of another individuality with whom he was in direct contact (such as Zarathustra or Master Jesus), who in pre-Christian times had recognized the Christ in the sun sphere and who would later prepare his body.

Speaking of one esoteric lesson held for a small group at the time of the Düsseldorf lecture cycle on the spiritual hierarchies in April 1909, Vreede said:[284] "Rudolf Steiner began with the words: 'My dear sisters and brothers! It is not the speaker who bears responsibility for this esoteric lesson.' He then illustrated how Zarathustra was initiated by Ahura Mazda; how Zarathustra stood before the great sun being. At that moment he was Zarathustra. It was a powerful experience: our great teacher, who had told us of the results of his research, now demonstrated to us how an ancient teacher and leader of humanity was able to reveal himself as inspiration once the path had been paved for him, as it were, by everything that had also inspired the cycle."[285] More generally, Rudolf Steiner himself said in an esoteric lesson: "With an exoteric presentation it is the speaker who bears the responsibility; with an esoteric presentation, it is the being whose voice he is, the being standing behind him."[286]

Elisabeth Vreede pointed out that Zarathustra (or Master Jesus) was able to "reveal himself as inspiration" in the esoteric lesson in Düsseldorf, once the lectures on the hierarchies had been given. It can be assumed, on the other hand, that the entire cycle most probably stood under his protection; that is, as the wisdom of Zarathustra or Master Jesus, its dissemination was supported and made possible by the master whom Rudolf Steiner allowed to speak through him in the esoteric lesson.

*

Rudolf Steiner never claimed the title of "master" for himself, and it is questionable whether his way of working was indeed that of a master in the classic sense—his advanced training and initiation notwithstanding. As Steiner once said, the masters of esoteric Christianity "are, as a rule, not historical personalities. They will, if necessary, occasionally incarnate in historical personalities, but that means that they sacrifice themselves to a certain extent. Their degree of consciousness is no longer compatible with any kind of self-interest; and in itself the preservation of a name constitutes an act of self-interest."[287] Steiner's work was not based on self-interest, but he worked in his own name and set great value on his name's being related to his work.

Elisabeth Vreede referred to Rudolf Steiner as "the first anthroposophist to pursue his research in human incarnation."[288] He did, in fact, develop anthroposophy on earth while undergoing a real incarnation, taking upon himself and living through a temporal destiny.[289] In contrast to Christian Rosenkreutz, Steiner had a very real "biography," from 1861 to 1925, with all the complex implications that involves; a biography that he himself described toward the end of his life in his autobiography as "the course of my life." No other master of esoteric Christianity had done anything like that before. Rudolf Steiner acted as *a person* and *with people* on whom he depended almost unconditionally in the fulfillment of his task or "mission." The success of his work depended largely on their acuteness, their inner maturity, and their readiness to take action—a fact that brought many tragic aspects to Rudolf Steiner's life.[290] At the same time, it made his work special, since it was not influenced by cosmic constellations (as the "sending" to Mars of Buddha through Rosenkreutz), but was carried out in the social realm. In the last lecture course on the Apocalypse, given to the Christian Community priests, Steiner described the "disorder" in the planetary system caused by Ahrimanic powers, among others, and the resultant catastrophes. He relied entirely on *humanity* to take on the task of counteracting such powers, out of a sense of responsibility and in freedom. ("... Only through strong human spirituality can a balance be generated to the disorder that will be contrived."[291])

Through his incarnation as Lazarus-John, Christian Rosenkreutz, an intimate pupil of Christ Jesus, was close to the events at the turning point of time. Master Jesus, who also accompanied Rudolf Steiner on his path (if in a more concealed way), took part in those events as the Solomon Jesus aspect. That means that Master Jesus was more intimately connected with the Christ mystery at the turning point of time than Christian Rosenkreutz was. For three years, Christ lived on earth in the body that Master Jesus had prepared.[292] Since then, Master Jesus has incarnated in every century, and has, from the fourteenth century on, guided the spiritual development of Central Europe together with Christian Rosenkreutz.[293] Rudolf Steiner was intimately connected with both these master individualities. Out of his absolute humanity on earth, his life of devotion and support for the "other," his respect of "Thou"—which had determined his biography since his childhood and adolescence—Steiner also had a profound connection with the specific qualities of the Nathan soul of Jesus.[294] The Nathan soul was with the Christ during his three earthly years, participating in all his actions and suffering, as well as in all the earthly-social processes into which the Christ being willingly entered as the only Divine being to incarnate in that way and suffer human death on earth. The Nathan soul also made possible Christ's community with the disciples, as the human center of Christ's mission on earth. The essence of the Nathan soul formed in Rudolf Steiner the foundation of the anthroposophic social community during his lifetime.[295]

Rudolf Steiner said of Benedictus (in the mystery dramas) that he had to "serve the spirit spheres"[296] with his counsel. Ita Wegman had the same impression of Rudolf Steiner when he died. Later, she communicated her feeling that Rudolf Steiner continued his work in the spiritual world as soon as he had passed the threshold. ("…and the other activity in the spiritual world began immediately. No further preparations were needed."[297]) Wegman also said that Rudolf Steiner's presence in the spiritual world was absolutely essential because of the knowledge (or earth experiences) that only he could take to the spiritual world:

> He was needed in the spiritual world; that was obvious. It was equally obvious that he had important knowledge to impart to the spiritual world; knowledge that only he could impart.[298]

During the last six months in his studio, Rudolf Steiner had clearly given Ita Wegman essential information about his life, on which she had taken brief notes. According to her notes, he told her that in his last lectures and writings, he had given everything "that people were able to take in," adding with regard to the present and future: "The main weight is on the spiritual world now. The dead need to be prepared for new earthly incarnation, as does the third hierarchy."[299] After he had given all he could in his earthly human incarnation, Rudolf Steiner's individuality was, already during his lifetime, redirected to cosmic dimensions for further activity.

About another conversation, Wegman wrote:

> My question was: "Why do we speak so little
> of Christ and so much of Michael?"
> Answer: "There is a mystery; Michael
> is my servant, he said."
> Not only Michael, but much higher powers spoke
> through him; Michael became the servant of his spirit.[300]
>
> Michael's concern about humanity:
> Michael's strength in Persephone;
> Michael powers in the Rosicrucians;
> Michael in *him*, not he serving Michael, but Michael
> serving him, because Christ's strength is in him.[301]

In his lectures Rudolf Steiner pointed out that since the sixteenth century "imprints" of the "I" of Christ have woven themselves into certain individualities on their journey. Rudolf Steiner was without doubt one of those individualities.[302] Over and above that, his whole essence, life, and work were imbued with the qualities of the Nathan Jesus; and he had access to the Solomon aspect of Jesus through his initiator, Master Jesus. Apart from that, Christian Rosenkreutz, the most intimate pupil of Christ Jesus, prepared anthroposophy as a deed of Michael and accompanied Rudolf Steiner on his journey.

*

The content of Rudolf Steiner's conversation with Ita Wegman, as written down by her, needs to be seen in that context. It explains why Rudolf Steiner, who was deeply devoted to his master Christian Rosenkreutz, said that anthroposophy, which he had researched and represented as the real language of Christ and Michael, encompassed a much wider area than Rosicrucianism.[303] Rudolf Steiner called Christian Rosenkreutz the "leader of the esoteric movement into the future." That implied that Christian Rosenkreutz had to ensure that the ancient, Christ-permeated mystery stream (from the West *and* the East) would find its way to the future in the Michael Age, which had started in 1879, and to the "light age." That transition took place successfully in Central Europe around 1879/1880, thanks to the help of Christian Rosenkreutz.[304] Anthroposophy was able to incarnate into that transition as a modern science of the spirit. *"It is our task today to receive the full stream of spiritual life that flows down to us from the heights."*[305]

Once anthroposophy had arrived on earth (not suddenly and completely, but gradually), Rosenkreutz, "the servant of Christ Jesus" and therefore of anthroposophy, continued to be of central importance to Rudolf Steiner and his work. Michael was the "guardian" of anthroposophy, as Ita Wegman wrote in accord with her teacher.[306] With the active help of Michael, who is always by his side, Christian Rosenkreutz and his stream ensure with their active support that the work begun by Rudolf Steiner in 1879 will continue. "The Doctor often said: 'Rosicrucianism must be taught as part of anthroposophy. Christian Rosenkreutz stands as an inspiration next to another whom he has chosen; we will never be able to keep the Goetheanum alive if the Rosicrucian stream, be it ever so concealed, is not intertwined with our anthroposophic movement'" (Ita Wegman[307]).

Rudolf Steiner said that Christian Rosenkreutz had suffered and endured much in the spiritual history of humanity, and that he would suffer more in the future—"that has to do with the great dangers that the truth will have to face in the future." The individuality of Rudolf Steiner will be fully included in the suffering and martyrdom still to be endured by Christian Rosenkreutz in connection with the future of spiritual life. The "truth" he referred to is anthroposophy.

*

2.

"Benedictus Deus Qui Dedit Nobis Signum"

The Admission Ritual for Leadership
in the Michael School

Rudolf Steiner's rose cross (obverse)

WHEN ITA WEGMAN wrote to Albert Steffen on August 21, 1925, five months after Rudolf Steiner's death, about her relationship with the First Class of the School for Spiritual Science, she mentioned a rose cross given to her by Rudolf Steiner. "Before his illness the Doctor gave me a small cross with small rubies set in roses, which he used to wear on a red ribbon around his neck. He put it on me with his own hands after we had performed a ritual act."[308] Rudolf Steiner's rose cross can be found as part of Ita Wegman's estate.[309] A few years later, on April 25, 1930, Ita Wegman spoke about the circumstances of the handing over of the cross, the preceding "ritual act," and their connection with the First Class during an Executive Council meeting with the general secretaries and delegates of the General Anthroposophical Society at the Goetheanum. "I also received his cross directly. He took it from his neck and put it on me with his own hands, saying: *'From this moment we will be there together for the Michael School.'*"[310]

"This meant that Rudolf Steiner, after performing the ritual act, and through the ritual of handing over the cross, admitted Ita Wegman to the Michael School as co-leader with joint responsibility. It is not known when the event took place. Ita Wegman mentioned no date, but she wrote to Albert Steffen that it was "before" Rudolf Steiner's illness, which first became apparent in late September 1924. There is sufficient reason to believe that Rudolf Steiner performed the ritual act and the passing on of the cross at the beginning of September 1924 (after his return from England) in his studio. In all class lessons Steiner held from September 6 onward, he emphasized Ita Wegman's special co-responsibility for the mantras of the ritual lessons and for the esoteric school.[311] People who were admitted to the First Class in September 1924 were ritually introduced by Steiner and Wegman together. "Admissions took place in the studio. I had to stand next to the Doctor; members were shown into the studio by Dr.

Wachsmuth. Dr. Steiner would ask applicants a few questions, and if they were to be admitted, Dr. Steiner would speak the following words: "If you are willing to remain faithful to the Michael School, take my hand. Take also Frau Dr. Wegman's hand, who will lead the Michael School together with me." (Ita Wegman[312])

Among the class members who were admitted in September 1924 was Wolfgang Moldenhauer, who described the admission procedure in exactly the same way in a letter to Kurt Franz David. "On November 5, 1924, I was admitted to the First Class by R. St. After the handshake and troth, he asked me to also take the hand of Frau Dr. Wegman who sat next to him as co-leader of the class."[313] In notes she took of an internal lecture, Ita Wegman wrote a brief summary about the changes in the affairs of the First Class in late summer 1924. "To me, he [Rudolf Steiner] said that people should know now that the class was the Michael School in the spiritual world. Of that school he was the leader and I was his assistant. It was my task to guard the mantras. Any member who wanted to pass a mantra on to another member had to consult me or him. This was an esoteric act, the beginning of a newly-to-be-introduced esotericism. At the same time it was arranged that during the admission procedure, applicants would hear the words: *This is the Michael School, which is led by me and Frau Wegman.*"[314]

*

Nothing further has so far been discovered about the handing over of the rose cross, especially about the preceding ritual act; although both (obviously associated) procedures were highly significant also for the class lessons, since from that time the first ritual elements (the "signs and seal of Michael") were introduced to the lessons. The unpublished minutes of an Executive Council meeting of November 29, 1930, reveal that a document about the performed ritual act was in Ita Wegman's possession. During the crisis of the Executive Council and the Society, Ita Wegman was forced again to confirm to her colleagues that Rudolf Steiner had indeed conferred joint responsibility for the class on her (nobody apart from Elisabeth Vreede believed her). She spoke about the ritual act: "[Tomorrow] I will take [bring] along the papers where he [Dr. Steiner] actually said it to me. I will read out the act where he said it."[315] Whether Ita Wegman actually went on to do that on November 30, 1930, is not documented.

Ita Wegman spoke of the joint performance of a ritual act that was sealed with the handing over of the rose cross. The "papers" recording the ritual act, or aspects of that act, form part of a comprehensive collection of mantras and esoteric exercises in Rudolf Steiner's handwriting, which she had received from him. The collection was preserved in full by the priest Emanuel Zeylmans van Emmichoven, and was published in 2009.[316] It includes a text in Rudolf Steiner's and Ita Wegman's hand-writing, covering several sheets. The text focuses on the rose cross and its transfer, culminating in the actual handing over; and contains ritual elements of a ritual antiphony between two people. Emanuel Zeylmans van Emmichoven wrote, "Because Ita Wegman wrote down Rudolf Steiner's oral instructions, it is possible for us to place the text, right into its individual images and personal statements, before our souls."[317] Considering all that is known about the context, there is little doubt that those sheets reflect or contain the ritual act performed by Rudolf Steiner with Ita Wegman in late summer 1924.[318] The text includes an evening and a morning meditation for Ita Wegman, both culminating in the meeting with a priest figure and the handing over of a rose cross. The mantric verses are associated with the esoteric training of the First Class, and end with a blessing on the meditating person who receives the rose cross from the priest figure—the "spirit guide." How much of the text was spoken in the performance of the act in Rudolf Steiner's studio can only be guessed; but one can assume that at least the antiphonal words about the rose cross and the concluding ritual blessing were spoken.

*

The evening meditation exercise for Ita Wegman begins with the review of one of the experiences of the day ("imagine an experience of the day in reverse order"[319]). This is followed by exact instructions given by Rudolf Steiner, taken down in her handwriting: a breathing exercise that is to be repeated seven times; an *IAO* exercise; and then the "rose cross imagination." The imagination was obviously meant to be linked to a mantra referring to the spiritual human form, and was to be meditated in relation to that form (focusing on heart and limb organization[320]):

> Primal Powers hold me
> Spirits of fire free me
> Spirits of light illumine me
> So that I reach toward spirit life
> So that I feel beings of soul
> So that I traverse uncertainties
> So that I stand above the abyss.[321]

If meditated accordingly, the Rose Cross imagination will convey strength and support to the human being from the third hierarchy (in the region of the heart), so that inner certainty can be gained for meeting the tasks and dangers of humanity with confidence.

That process of strengthening, affirmation, and empowerment (or encouragement) was to be followed by further deepened concentration—full inner immersion into the Christ Mystery with the mantra:

> In me let Christ live
> And change my breath
> And warm the course of my blood
> And shine into my soul being.[322]

Rudolf Steiner's transcript of the evening meditation ends with the instruction, "maintain inner poise." In the margin of the page Steiner had added behind a square bracket, "White robe. Red belt and pendant. Red headband. I: *Ave frater* [Hail thee, brother]. He: *rosae et aureae* [of the rosy and golden]. I: *crucis* [cross]. He: *Benedictus deus qui dedit nobis signum* [Blessed be God who gave us the sign]."

What Steiner had written down and passed on to Ita Wegman was obviously a summary, which served as a reminder. He would have specified the inner process to her verbally in much more detail. According to Wegman's notes, the "rose cross" had to be retrieved from the heart of the meditating person, where it had previously been "placed" after the Christ meditation. Wegman did not specify in her notes whether the rose cross meditation on the mantric verse "Primal Powers hold me…" was to be experienced as the spiritual configuration of a rose cross (and be held in the heart, as the central human organ). The overall movement seems to indicate, however, that the rose cross had to be created, or reproduced, mantrically and internalized during the exercise.

After the rose cross had been "retrieved" from the heart, it had to be carried imaginatively up a mountain, "step by step." On the mountain peak an encounter should take place in the imagination with a figure ("person") in priestly ritual vestment (with white robe, red stole, red band around the neck, and red belt; the colors of Christian Rosenkreutz, white and red, in the *Chymical Wedding*.) Ita Wegman wrote about that meeting:

> One has to hand the rose cross over to that person with the words: *Ave frater* and sense the other's response: *Rosae and aureae*. With devotion one answers: *crucis*. The other speaks: *Benedictus deus qui dedit nobis signum*.

After the imaginative experience of such a meeting; that is, the joint, antiphonal speaking of the words, "Hail thee, brother of the rosy and golden cross"; the blessing of God through the

priestly figure; and the handing over to that figure of the rose
cross that has been carried up, the meditating person turns back.
"Then the imagination that one leaves the other again. After
that, allow a sense of calm to enter into the soul. Empty the
mind." The rose cross remains on the mountain.

*

As a reminder for the morning meditation Rudolf Steiner
wrote simply:

> Imagination on the mountain. Being received.
> Holding up ♀ [the rose cross]
>
> May my head condense the spirit of worlds
> Extracting for me the living light of thoughts
> May my throat parch the breath of soul
> Infusing it with spirit word meaning
> Live in my *heart*, you, my spirit guide
> There to unite me with you
> That I move live weave in spirit soul life.

Ita Wegman added more details to her notes:

> Imagine in the morning:
> That one has climbed up the mountain again; that one meets
> the same person in the same robe; that the figure gives back
> the rose cross given to him [her] on the previous evening.

> Imagination to be meditated, kneeling down:

> 1. May my head condense the spirit of worlds
> Extracting for me the living light of thoughts
> 2. May my throat parch the breath of soul
> Infusing it with spirit word meaning

3. Live in my *heart*, you, my spirit guide
There to unite me with you
That I move live weave in spirit soul life!

1. Feel the head – the thinking – like a stone
2. The throat like a parched plant
3. Concentration on the heart while meditating the above.

Now meditate that the person gives back the rose cross and places the right hand on top of the left; then both hands on the forehead, speaking the words, *"Benedictus deus qui dedit nobis signum."*

Empty the mind again.

The meditation of the pupil climbing the mountain again, which is carried out while kneeling, culminates in the spiritual union with the priestly figure in the heart, the human organ of destiny. ("Live in my heart, you, my spirit guide, there to unite me with you.") After that, as Ita Wegman's notes suggest, the "spirit guide" gives [returns] the rose cross to the pupil, with a blessing and laying of hands on the pupil's forehead.

"And I ... received his cross directly. He took it from his neck and put it on me with his own hands, saying: *'From this moment we will be there together for the Michael School.'"* With those words, Ita Wegman described how Rudolf Steiner handed over the cross to her directly after performing the ritual act. "In united effort of soul,"[323] united in the spirit ("there to unite me with you"), Rudolf Steiner wanted to work actively for the Michael School with Ita Wegman, accompanying and supporting her on her inner path, but also needing her assistance.[324]

"Live in my *heart*, you, my spirit guide/ there to unite me with you/ that I move live weave in spirit soul life!" These are the final words of the mantra that the pupil meditated imaginatively, while kneeling down, just before the final handing over of the rose cross. The same esoteric motif of assistance and union appeared at the end of another mantric verse that Rudolf Steiner had already given Ita Wegman in September 1923, a year before the ritual for the First Class, asking her to meditate it every evening:

> Ever shining, supreme light:
> To you I entrust my soul.
> May the light of my soul weave
> With the weaving light of worlds.
> As light I feel,
> Light in the smallest point;
> Light that widens boundlessly.
> Pure transparent light am I.
> I seize hold of the spirit world
> At the end of my soul of light,
> I hold the spirit world
> With my arms of light;
> I sense your presence,
> You want to carry me
> To worlds of light and spirit.[325]

*

Am Abend : Erst ein Tageserlebnis rückwärts vorstellen.
Dann Imagination des
✝

Urkräfte haltet mich
Geister des Feuers befreiet mich
Geister des Lichtes erleuchtet mich
~~Dann ich~~ ~~Ungewissheit~~
~~Zuversicht~~

Denn ich greife nach Geisterfein
Denn ich fühle die Seelenwesen
Denn ich schreite über Ungewissheiten
Denn ich gehe über Abgründen

dann versuchen ganz sich vertiefen in :

In mir lebe der Christus
Und wandle meinen Atem
Und wärme meines Blutes Lauf
Und leuchte meinem Seelenwesen.

Ruhiges Verharren in sich :

Am Morgen :

Imagination auf Berg. Empfangenwerden.
Vorstellen ✝

Mein Haupt erhärte Wellengeist
~~Und~~ Befreie ~~mir~~ ~~daraus~~ Gedankenleibesleben
~~Meine Kehle verdorre~~ ~~Luftesseele~~
Ergreise in sie geisteswortes sinn
Mein Herz bewohne du mein Geistesführer
Da Eine du mich mit Dir
Dass ich schwebe lebe webe im Geistesseelenfein

weisses Gewand. Roter Gürtel und
Gefänge. Rotes Stirnband.

⚜ Ave pater
G Tos eae et aureae
⚜ crucis
⚜ Benedictus deus qui dedit
nobis signum

Rudolf Steiner's notes

(Meditation

*Am Abend Rückschau
über das am Tage vorge-
fallene in Bilderform
Einen tiefen Atemzug holen
dieser Atem dann gehen lassen
vom Nasenwurzel über das
Haupt bis zum hinteren Teil
des Nackens (J)
Den Atem halten dann gehen
lassen vom Nacken durch
die Ärme in die Handpalme
(A) Rechter Handpalme auf
das linke (O) dann den
Atemzug durch den Solar
Plexus gehen lassen.
(7 mal, wiederholen)*

Ita Wegman's notes

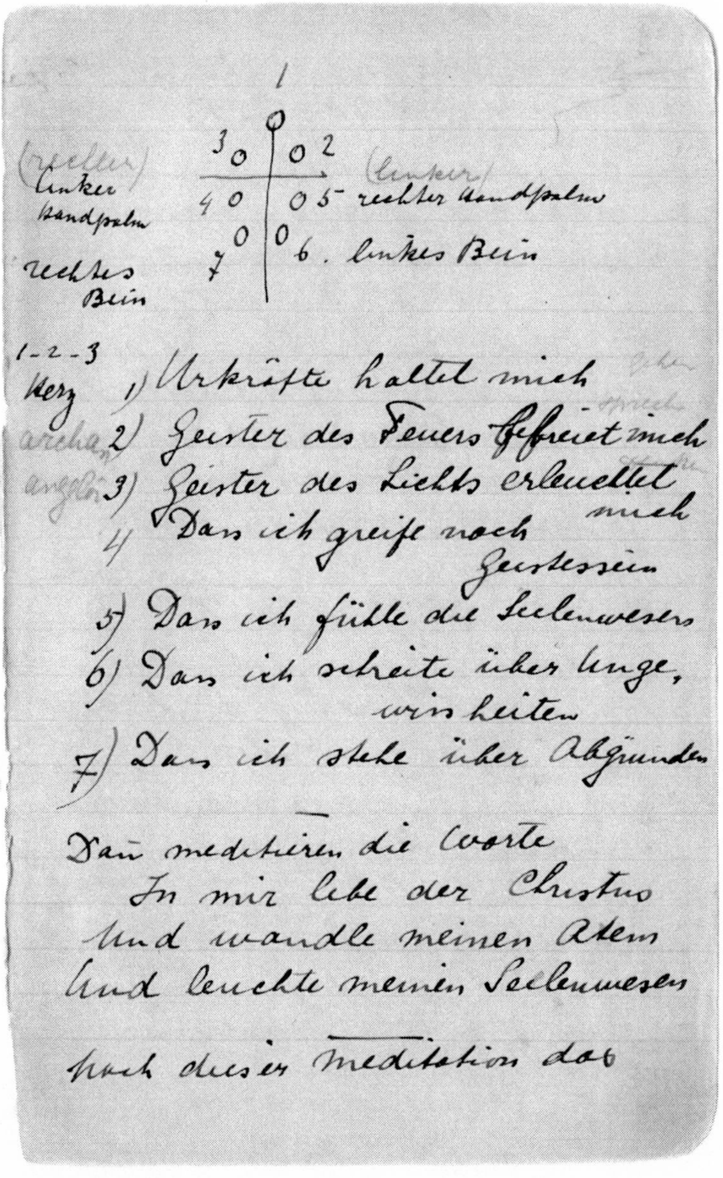
1
3 0 | 0 2 (linker)
(rechter)
linker
Handpalm
4 0 | 0 5 rechter Handpalm
7 0 | 0 6. linkes Bein
rechtes
Bein

1-2-3
Herz 1) Urkräfte haltet mich
archai 2) Geister des Feuers befreiet mich
angeloi 3) Geister des Lichts erleuchtet mich
4 Dass ich greife noch Geistessein
5) Dass ich fühle die Seelenwesen
6) Dass ich schreite über Ungewissheiten
7) Dass ich stehe über Abgründen

Dann meditieren die Worte
In mir lebe der Christus
Und wandle meinen Atem
Und leuchte meinen Seelenwesen

Nach dieser Meditation das

Ita Wegman's notes

Dañ die weitere Imagination
dass man diesen andern
verlässt
Daraufhin Ruhe eintreten
lassen in der Seele
Leer machen das Bewusstsein

—

Morgens imaginieren:
dass man wieder den Berg
aufgestiegen ist, dass man
die gleiche Person mit der
gleichen Gewandung begegnet
und dass diese das Rosen-
kreuz wieder zurückgibt
das man ihm den vorigen
Abend gegeben hat
Imaginieren, dass man
kniend das folgende medit.
Mein Haupt erhärte Weltengeist
Befreie mir daraus Gedankenhelles Leben
Meine Kehle verdorre Luftesseele
Ergiesse in sie Gisteswortesinn
Mein Herz bewohne du mein Geistesfühl
Da eine Du mich mit Dir
Dass ich schwebe lebe webe in Gistes-
seelensein

Ita Wegman's notes

RosenKreuz aus dem Herzen
in dem man er vorher gelegt
hat heraus holen
Daraufhin muss man die
Imagination haben das.
man Schritt für Schritt
zu einem Berg hinaufsteigt
den RosenKreuz tragend.
Auf der Bergspitze begegnet
man eine Person in einem
weisen Gewand mit roten
Stola, roten Gurt und roten
Band um dem Hals
An diesen Person gibt man
den Rosenkreuz und sagt
zu ihm „Ave frater"
Man fühlt, dass der andere
antwortet „Rosae et aurae
man antwortet mit devotion
zurück. Crucis"
Der andere sagt: „Benedictus
Deus qui dedit nobis Signum
qui
✝

Ita Wegman's notes

der denken

1/ Fühlen das Haupt (wie ein Stein.

2/ Die Kelle wie eine verdorrte Pflanze

3) Concentration auf das Herz bei der meditation des vorangegangenen

Nun ist zu meditieren dass diese Person den Rosen kreuz zurückgibt; dass er der rechte Hand auf den linken legt, dass beide Hände auf den Stirn legt und die folgenden Worte spricht: „Benedictus Deus qui dedit notis signum" Wieder leeres Bewustsein machen

Ita Wegman's notes

3.

Fama Fraternitatis

(c. 1610-1612)

translated by Thomas Vaughan (1652)

The first edition of the *Fama* was published in Cassel, "not later than August" 1614. It was titled: *Universal and General Reformation of the Whole Wide World; together with the Fama Fraternitatis of the Laudable Order of the Rosy Cross, written to all the learned and Rulers of Europe; also a short Reply sent by Herr Haselmeyer, for which he was seized by the Jesuits and put in irons on a Galley; Now put forth in print and communicated to all true Hearts. Printed at Cassel by Wilhelm Wessel, 1614.*

One of the earliest, if not the earliest ms. English versions of the *Fame and Confession* is the so-called "Crawford Manuscript" of 1633, preserved in the private library of the Earls of Crawford and Balcarres. On the flyleaf is written, "Balcarres, 1633," and the writer was Sir David Lindsay, created first Lord Balcarres, June 1633, died 1641. He is known to have had a profound interest in alchemy, and "left in ms. several volumes of transcripts and translations from the works of the Rosecrucians."

This present translation, dated 1652 and ascribed to Thomas Vaughan, is based to some extent at least upon the "Crawford Manuscript."

—Paul M. Allen

FAMA FRATERNITATIS

Oder

Brüderschafft des hochlöblichen
Ordens des R: C:

an
Die Häupter, Stende vnd Gelehrten
Europæ

Wir die brüder der fraternitet des R: C: ...
... Famam
... maining ...
...

Fama Fraternitatis, manuscript, c. 1610–1612
Wellcome Historical Medical Library, London

We, the Bretheren of the *Fraternity* of the R.C. bestow our Greeting, Love and Prayers upon each and everyone who reads this our *Fama* of Christian intent.

Seeing the only Wise and Merciful God in these latter days hath poured out so richly his mercy and goodness to Mankind, wherby we do attain more and more to the perfect knowledge of his Son Jesus Christ and *Nature*, that justly we may boast of the happy time, wherein there is not only discovered unto us the half part of the World, which was heretofore unknown & hidden, that he hath also made manifest unto us many wonderful, and never-heretofore seen, Works and Creatures of *Nature*, and more over hath raised men, indued with great Wisdom, which might partly renew and reduce all Arts (in this our Age spotted and imperfect) to perfection; so that finally Man might thereby understand his own Nobleness and Worth, and why he is called *Microcosmus*, and how far his knowledg extendeth in Nature.

Although the rude World herewith will be but little pleased, but rather smile and scoff thereat; also the Pride and Covetousness of the Learned is so great, it will not suffer them to agree together; but were they united, they might out of all those things which in this our Age God doth so richly bestow upon us, collect *Librum Naturae*, or a perfect Method of all Arts: but such is their opposition, that they still keep, and are loth to leave the old course, esteeming *Porphiry*, *Aristotle*, and *Galen*, yea and that which hath put a meer shew of learning, more than the clear and manifested Light and Truth; who if they were now living, with much joy would leave their erroneous Doctrines. But here is too great weakness for such a great Work: And although in *Theologie*, *Physic*, and the *Mathematic*, the Truth doth manifest it self; nevertheless the old Enemy by his subtilty and craft doth shew himself in hindering every good purpose by his Instruments and contentious wavering people. To such an intent of a general

Reformation, the most godly and highly illuminated Father, our Brother. *C. R.* a German, the chief and original of our Fraternity, hath much and long time laboured, who by reason of his poverty (although descended of Noble Parents) in the fifth year of his age was placed in a Cloyster, where he had learned indifferently the *Greek* and *Latin* Tongues, who (upon his earnest desire and request) being yet in his growing years, was associated to a Brother, *P. A. L.* who had determined to go to the Holy Land.

Although this Brother dyed in *Ciprus*, and so never came to *Jerusalem*, yet our Brother C. R. did not return, but shipped himself over, and went to *Damasco*, minding from thence to go to Jerusalem; but by reason of the feebleness of his body he remained still there, and by his skill in Physick he obtained much favour with the *Turks*: In the mean time he became by chance acquainted with the Wise men of *Damasco* in *Arabia*, and beheld what great Wonders they wrought, and how *Nature* was discovered unto them; hereby was that high and noble Spirit of Brother C. R. so stired up, that *Jerusalem* was not so much now in his mind as *Damasco*; also he could not bridle his desires any longer, but made a bargain with the *Arabians*, that they should carry him for a certain sum of money to *Damasco*; he was but of the age of sixteen years when he came thither, yet of a strong Dutch constitution; there the Wise received him (as he himself witnesseth) not as a stranger, but as one whom they had long expected, they called him by his name, and shewed him other secrets out of his Cloyster, whereat he could not but mightily wonder: He learned there better the *Arabian* Tongue; so that the year following he translated the Book *M.* into good *Latin*, which he afterwards brought with him. This is the place where he did learn his Physick, and his Mathematicks, whereof the World hath just cause to rejoyce, if there were more Love, and less Envy. After three years he returned again with good consent, shipped himself over *Sinus Arabicus* into *Egypt*, where he remained not long, but only took better notice there of the Plants and Creatures; he sailed over the whole *Mediterranean*

Sea for to come unto *Fez*) where the *Arabians* had directed him. And it is a great shame unto us, that wise men, so far remote th'one from th'other, should not only be of one opinion, hating all contentious Writings, but also be so willing and ready under the seal of secrecy to impart their secrets to others.

Every year the *Arabians* and *Afiricans* do send one to another, inquiring one of another out of their Arts, if happily they had found out some better things, or if Experience had weakened their Reasons. Yearly there came something to light, whereby the *Mathematica*, *Physic* and *Magic* (for in those are they of *Fez* most skilful) were amended; as there is nowadays in *Germany* no want of learned Men, *Magicians, Cabalists, Physicians,* and *Philosophers*, were there but more love and kindness among them, or that the most part of them would not keep their secrets close only to themselves. At *Fez* he did get acquaintance with those which are commonly called the Elementary Inhabitants, who revealed unto him many of their secrets: As we *Germans* likewise might gather together many things, if there were the like unity, and desire of searching out of secrets amongst us.

Of these of *Fez* he often did confess, that their *Magia* was not altogether pure, and also that their *Cabala* was defiled with their Religion; but notwithstanding he knew how to make good use of the same, and found still more better grounds of his Faith, altogether agreeable with the Harmony of the whole World, and wonderfully impressed in all Periods of times, and thence proceedeth that fair Concord, that as in every several kernel is contained a whole good tree or fruit, so likewise is included in the little body of Man the whole great World, whose Religion, policy, health, members, nature, language, words and works, are agreeing, sympathizing, and in equal tune and melody with God, Heaven and Earth; and that which is dis-agreeing with them, is error, falsehood, and of the Devil, who alone is the first, middle, and last cause of strife, blindness, and darkness in the World: Also, might one examine all and several persons upon the Earth, he should find that which is good and right, is always agreeing with it self; but all the rest is spotted with a thousand erroneous conceits.

After two years Brother C. R. departed the City *Fez*, and sailed with many costly things into *Spain*, hoping well, he himself had so well and so profitably spent his time in his travel, that the learned in *Europe* would highly rejoyce with him, and begin to rule, and order all their Studies, according to those sound and sure Foundations. He therefore conferred with the Learned in *Spain*, shewing unto them the Errors of our Arts, and how they might be corrected, and from whence they should gather the true *Inditia* of the Times to come, and wherein they ought to agree with those things that are past; also how the faults of the Church and the whole *Philosopia Moralis* was to be amended: He shewed them new Growths, new Fruits, and Beasts, which did concord with old *Philosophy*, and prescribed them new *Axiomata*, whereby all things might fully be restored: But it was to them a laughing matter; and being a new thing unto them, they feared that their great Name should be lessened, if they should now again begin to learn and acknowledg their many years Errors, to which they were accustomed, and wherewith they had gained them enough: Who-so loveth unquietness, let him be reformed.

The same Song was also sang to him by other Nations, the which moved him the more (because it happened to him contrary to his expectation.) being then ready bountifully to impart all his Arts and Secrets to the Learned, if they would have but undertaken to write the true and infallible *Axiomata*, out of all Faculties, Sciences and Arts, and whole *Nature*, as that which he knew would direct them, like a Globe, or Circle, to the onely middle Point, and *Centrum*, and (as it is usual among the *Arabians*) it should only serve to the wise and learned for a Rule, that also there might be a Society in *Europe*, which might have Gold, Silver, and precious Stones, sufficient for to bestow them on Kings, for their necessary uses, and lawful purposes: with which such as be Governors might be brought up, for to learn all that which God hath suffered Man to know, and thereby to be enabled in all times of need to give their counsel unto those that seek it, like the Heathen Oracles: verily we must confess that the world in those days was already big with those great Commotions, laboring to be delivered of them; and did bring forth painful, worthy men, who brake with all force through Darkness and Barbarism, and left us who succeeded to follow them: and assuredly they have been the uppermost point in *Trygono igneo*, whose flame now should be more and more brighter, and shall undoubtedly give to the World the last Light.

Such a one likewise hath *Theophrastus*[1] been in Vocation nevertheless hath he diligently read over the Book *M.*: whereby his sharp *ingenium* was exalted; but this man was also hindered in his course by the multitude of the learned and wise-seeming men, that he was never able peaceably to confer with others of his Knowledg and Understanding he had of *Nature*. And therefore in his writing he rather mocked these busie bodies, and doth now shew them altogether what he was; yet nevertheless there is found with him well grounded the aforenamed *Harmonia*, which without doubt he had imparted to the Learned, if he had not found them rather worthy of subtil vexation, than to be instructed in greater Arts and Sciences; he then with a free and careless life lost his time, and left unto the World their foolish pleasures.

But that we do not forget our loving Father, Brother *C. R.* he after many painful Travels, and his fruitless true Instructions, returned again into *Germany*, the which he (by reason of the alterations[2] which were shortly to come, and of the strange and dangerous contentions) heartily loved: There, although he could have bragged with his Art, but specially of the transmutations of Metals; yet did he esteem more Heaven, and the Citizens thereof, Man, then all vain glory and pomp.

Nevertheless he builded a fitting and neat habitation, in the which he ruminated his Voyage, and Philosophy, and reduced them together in a true Memorial. In this house he spent a great time in the *Mathematicks*, and made many fine Instruments, (*ex omnibus hujus artis partibus*, whereof there is but little remaining to us, as hereafter you shall understand, After five years came again into his mind the wished for Reformation; and in regard he doubted of the ayd and help of others, although he himself was painful, lusty, and unwearisome, he undertook, with some few adjoyned with him, to attempt the same: wherefore he desired to that end, to have out of his first Cloyster (to the which he bare a great affection) three of his Brethren, Brother *G. V.* Brother *J. A.* and Brother *J. O.* who besides that, they had some more knowledg in the Arts, than at that time many others had, he did binde those three unto himself, to be faithful, diligent, and secret; as also to commit carefully to writing, all that which he should direct and instruct them in, to the end that those which were to come, and through especial Revelation should be received into this Fraternity, might not be deceived of the least sillable and word.

After this manner began the Fraternity of the *Rosie Cross*; first, by four persons onely, and by them was made the Magical Language and writing, with a large Dictionary, which we yet dayly use to Gods praise and glory, and do finde great wisdom therein; they made also the first part of the Book *M*: but in respect that that labor was too heavy, and the unspeakable concourse of the sick hindred them, and also whilst his new building (called *Sancti spiritus*) was now finished, they concluded to draw and receive yet others more into their Fraternity; to this end was chosen brother *R. C.* his deceased fathers brothers son, brother *B.* a skilful Painter, *G.* and *P. D.* their Secretary, all *Germains* except *J. A.* so in all they were eight in number, all batchelors and of vowed virginity, by those was collected a book or volumn of all that which man can desire, wish, or hope for.

Although we do now freely confess, that the World is much amended within an hundred years, yet we are assured, that our *Axiomata* shall unmovably remain unto the Worlds End, and also the world in her highest & last Age shall not attain to see any thing else; for our *Rota* takes her beginning from that day when God spake *Fiat*, and shall end when he shall speak *Pereat*; yet Gods Clock striketh every minute, where ours scarce striketh perfect hours. We also stedfastly beleeve, that if our Brethren and Fathers had lived in this our present and clear light, they would more roughly have handled the Pope, *Mahomet*, Scribes, Artists, and Sophisters, and had shewed themselves more helpful, not simply with sighs, and wishing of their end and consummation.

When now these eight Brethren had disposed and ordered all things in such manner, as there was not now need of any great labour, and also that every one was sufficiently instructed, and able perfectly to discourse of secret and manifest Philosophy, they would not remain any longer together, but as in the beginning they had agreed, they separated themselves into several Countries, because that not only their *Axiomata* might in secret be more profoundly examined by the learned, but that they themselves, if in some Country or other they observed any thing, or perceived some Error, they might inform one another of it.

Their Agreement was this; First, That none of them should profess any other thing, than to cure the sick, and that *gratis*. 2. None of the Posterity should be constrained to wear one certain kind of habit, but therein to follow the custom of the Country. 3. That every year upon the day *C.*[3] they should meet together at the house *S. Spiritus*, or write the cause of his absence. 4. Every Brother should look about for a worthy person, who after his disease might succeed him. 5. The word *C. R.* should be their Seal, Mark, and Character. 6. The Fraternity should remain secret one hundred years. These six Articles they bound themselves one to another to keep: and five of the Brethren departed, only the Brethren *B.* and *D.* remained with the Father *Fra: R. C.* a whole year: when these likewise departed, then remained by him his Cousen and Brother *J. O.* so that he hath all the days of his life with him two of his Brethren. And although that as yet the Church was not cleansed, nevertheless we knew that they did think of her, and what with longing desire they looked for: Every

year they assembled together with joy, and made a full resolu-
tion of that which they had done; there must certainly have been
great pleasure, to hear truly and without invention related and
rehearsed all the Wonders which God hath poured out here and
there through the World. Everyone may hold it out for certain,
that such persons as were sent, and joyned together by God, and
the Heavens; and chosen out of the wisest of men, as have lived
in many Ages, did live together above all others in highest Unity,
greatest Secrecy, and most kindness one towards another.

After such a most laudable sort they did spend their lives; and
although they were free from all diseases and pain, yet notwithstanding they could not live and pass their time appointed of God.
The first of this Fraternity which dyed, and that in *England*, was *J.
O.* as Brother *C.* long before had foretold him; he was very expert,
and well learned in *Cabala*, as his Book called *H.* witnesseth: In
England he is much spoken of, and chiefly because he cured a
young Earl of *Norfolk* of the Leprosie. They had concluded, that
as much as possibly could be their burial place should be kept
secret, as at this day it is not known unto us what is become of
some of them, yet every ones place was supplyed with a fit successor; but this we will confesse publickly by these presents to
the honour of God, That what secret soever we have learned out
of the Book *M.* (although before our eyes we behold the image
and *pattern* of all the world) yet are there not shewn unto us our
misfortunes, nor hour of death, the which only is known to God
himself, who thereby would have us keep in a continual readiness;
but hereof more in our Confession, where do we set down 37
Reasons wherefore we now do make known our Fraternity, and
proffer such high Mysteries freely, and without constraint and
reward: also do we promise more gold than both the Indies bring
to the· King of *Spain*; for *Europe* is with child and wil bring forth
a strong child, who shall stand in need of a great godfathers gift.

After the death of *J. O.* Brother *R. C.* rested not, but as soon
as he could, called the rest together, (and as we suppose) then his
grave was made; although hitherto we (who were the latest) did

not know when our loving father *R. C.* died, and had no more
but the bare names of the beginners, and all their successors to
us; yet there came into our memory, a secret, which through
dark and hidden words, and speeches of the 100 years, Brother
A. the successor of *D.* (who was of the last and second row and
succession, and had lived amongst many of us), did impart unto
us of the third row and succession; otherwise we must confess,
that after the death of the said *A.* none of us had in any manner
known any thing of Brother *R. C.* and of his first fellow-breth-
ren, than that which was extant of them in our Philosophical
Bibliotheca, amongst which our *Axiomata* was held for the
chiefest, *Rota Mundi*,[4] for the most artificial, and *Protheus* the
most profitable. Likewise we do not certainly know if these of
the second row have been of the like wisdom as the first, and if
they were admitted to all things. It shall be declared hereafter to
the gentle Reader, not onely what we have heard of the burial of
R. C. but also made manifest publickly by the foresight, suffer-
ance and commandment of God, whom we most faithfully obey,
that if we shall be answered discreetly and Christian-like, we
will not be afraid to set forth publickly in Print, our names, and
sirnarnes, our meetings, or any thing else that may be required
at our hands.

Now the true and fundamental relation of the finding out of
the high illuminated man of God, *Fra: C. R. C.* is this: After
that *A.* in *Gallic Narbonensi* was deceased, then succeeded
in his place, our loving Brother *N. N.* this man after he had
repaired unto us to take the solemn oath of fidelity and secrecy,
he informed us *bona fide*, That *A.* had comforted him in telling
him, that this Fraternity should ere long not remain so hidden,
but should be to all the whole *German* Nation helpful, needful,
and commendable; of the which he was not in any wise in his
estate ashamed of. The year following after he had performed his
School right, and was minded now to travel, being for that purpose sufficiently provided with *Fortunatus* purse, he thought (he
being a good *Architect*) to alter something of his building, and to

make it more fit: in such renewing he lighted upon the memorial
Table which was cast of brasse, and containeth all the names of
the brethren, with some few other things; this he would transfer
in another more fitting vault: for where or when *Fra: R. C.* died,
or in what country he was buried, was by our predecessors concealed and unknown unto us. In this Table stuck a great naile
somewhat strong, so that when he was with force drawn out, he
took with him an indifferent big stone out of the thin wall, or
plaistering of the hidden door, and so unlooked for uncovered
the door; wherefore we did with joy and longing throw down
the rest of the wall, and cleared the door, upon which that was
written in great letters, *Post 120 annos patebo*[5] with the year of
the Lord o[6] under it; therefore we gave God thanks and let it rest
that same night, because first we would overlook our *Rotam*:
but we refer our selves again to the Confession, for what we
here publish is done for the help of those that are worthy, but
to the unworthy (God willing) it will be small profit: For like
as our door was after so many years wonderfully discovered,
also there shall be opened a door to *Europe* (when the wall is
removed) which already doth begin to appear, and with great
desire is expected of many.

In the morning following we opened the door, and there
appeared to our sight a Vault of seven sides and corners, every
side five foot broad, and the height of eight foot; Although the
Sun never shined in this Vault, nevertheless it was enlightned
with another sun, which had learned this from the Sun, and was
scituated in the upper part in the Center of the sieling; in the
midst, in stead of a Tomb-stone, was a round Altar covered over
with a plate of brass, and thereon this engraven:

A. C. R. C. Hoc universi compen-
dium unius mili sepulchrum feci.[7]

Round about the first Circle or Brim stood,
Jesus mihi omnia.[8]

In the middle were four figures, inclosed in circles, whose circumscription was,

1. *Nequaquam vacuum.*
2. *Legis Jugum.*
3. *Libertas Evangelij.*
4. *Dei gloria intacta.*[9]

This is all clear and bright, as also the seven sides and the two *Heptagoni*: so we kneeled altogether down, and gave thanks to the sole wise, sole mighty and sole eternal God, who hath taught us more than all mens wit could have found out, praised be his holy name. This Vault we parted in three parts, the upper part or sieling, the wall or side, the ground or floor.

Of the upper part you shall understand no more of it at this time, but that it was divided according to the seven sides in the triangle, which was in the bright center; but what therein is contained, you shall God willing (that are desirous of our society) behold the same with your own eys; but every side or wall is parted into ten squares, every one with their several figures and sentences, as they are truly shewed, and set forth *Concentratum* here in our book.

The bottom again is parted in the triangle, but because therein is discribed the power and rule of the inferior Governors, we leave to manifest the same, for fear of the abuse by the evil and ungodly world. But those that are provided and stored with the heavenly Antidote, they do without fear or hurt, tread on, and bruise the head of the old and evil serpent, which this our age is well fitted for: every side or wall had a door for a chest, wherein there lay divers things, especially all our books, which otherwise we had, besides the *Vocabular* of *Theoph: Par. Ho,*[10] and these which daily unfalsifieth we do participate.[11] Herein also we found our Father's *Itinerarium*, and *vitam*, whence this relation for the most part is taken. In another chest were looking-glasses of divers virtues, as also in other places were little bells, burning lamps, & chiefly wonderful artificial Songs; generally al done to that end, that if it should happen after many hundred years, the Order or Fraternity should come to nothing, they might by this onely Vault be restored again.

Now as yet we had not seen the dead body of our careful and wise Father, we therefore removed the Altar aside, there we lifted up a strong plate of brass, and found a fair and worthy body, whole and unconsumed, as the same is here lively counterfeited, with all the Ornaments and Attires; in his hand he held a parchment book, called T,[12] the which next unto the Bible, is our greatest treasure, which ought not lightly to be delivered to the censure of the world. At the end of this book standeth this following *Elogium*:[13]

Granum pectori Jesu insitum.

C. Ros. C. ex nobili atque splendida Germaniae R.C. familia oriundus, vir sui seculi divinis revoelationibus subtilissimis imaginationibus, indefessis laboribus ad coelestia, atque humana mysteria; arcanave admissus postquam suam (quam Arabico, & Africano itineribus Collegerat) plusquam regiam, atque imperatoriam Gazam suo seculo nondum convenientem, posteritati eruendam custo divisset & jam suarum Artium, ut & nominis, fides acconjunctissimos herides instituisset, mundum minutum omnibus motibus magno illi respondentem fabricasset hocque tandem preteritarurn, praesentium, & futurarum, rerum compendia extracto, centenario major non morbo (quem ipse nunquam corpors expert us erat, nunquam alios iniestare sinebat) ullo pellente sed spiritu Dei evocante, illuminatam animam (inter Fratrum amplexus & ultima oscula) fidelissimo creatori Deo reddidisset, Pater dilectissimus, Fra: suavissimus, praeceptor fidelissimus amicus integerimus, a suis ad 120 annos hic absconditus est.

Underneath they had subscribed themselves,

1 *Fra: I. A. Fr. C. H. electione Fraternitatis caput.*[14]
2 *Fr: G. V. M. P. C.*
3 *Fra: R. C. Iunior haeres S. Spiritus.*
4 *Fra: B.M.P.A. Pictor & Architectus.*
5 *Fr: G. G. M. P. I. Cabalista.*

Secundi Circuli.

1 *Fra: P. A. Successor, Fr: I. O. Mathematicus.*
2 *Fra: A. Successor Fra. P. D.*
3 *Fra: R. Successor patris C. R. C. cum Christo triumphantis.*

At the end was written,

Ex Deo nascimur, in Jesu morimur, per Spiritum Sanctum reviviscimus.[15]

At that time was already dead Brother *I. O.* and *Fra: D* but their burial place where is it to be found? we doubt not but our *Fra: Senior* hath the same, and some especial thing layd in Earth, and perhaps likewise hidden: we also hope that this our Example will stir up others more deligently to enquire after their names (whom we have therefore published) and to search for the place of their burial; for the most part of them, by reason of their practice and physick, are yet known, and praised among very old folks; so might perhaps our *Gaza* be enlarged, or at least be better cleared.

Concerning *Minutum Mundum*, we found it kept in another little Altar, truly more finer than can be imagined by any understanding man; but we will leave him undescribed, untill we shal truly be answered upon this our true hearted *Famam*; and so we have covered it again with the plates, and set the altar thereon, shut the door, and made it sure, with all our seals; besides by instruction and command of our *Rota*, there are come to sight some books, among which is contained *M.* (which were made

in stead of household care by the praise-worthy *M. P.*) Finally
we departed the one from the other, and left the natural heirs in
possession of our Jewels. And so we do expect the answer and
judgment of the learned, or unlearned.

Howbeit we know after a time there will now be a general
reformation, both of divine and humane things, according to
our desire, and the expectation of others: for it's fitting, that
before the rising of the Sun, there should appear and break forth
Aurora, or some clearness, or divine light in the sky; and so
in the mean time some few, which shall give their names, may
joyn together, thereby to increase the number and respect of our
Fraternity, and make a happy and wished for beginning of our
Philosophical Canons, prescribed to us by our brother *R. C.* and
be partakers with us of our treasures (which never can fail or
be wasted) in all humility, and love to be eased of this worlds
labor, and not walk so blindly in the knowledge of the wonderful works of God.

But that also every Christian may know of what Religion and
belief we are, we confess to have the knowledge of Jesus Christ
(as the same now in these last days, and chiefly in *Germany*, most
clear and pure is professed, and is nowadays cleansed and voyd
of all swerving people, Hereticks, and false Prophets,) in certain
and noted Countries maintained, defended and propagated: Also
we use two Sacraments, as they are instituted with all *Formes* and
Ceremonies of the first renewed Church. In *Politia* we acknowl-
edge the *Roman* Empire and *Quartam Monarchiam*[16] for our
Christian head; albeit we know what alterations be at hand, and
would fain impart the same with all our hearts, to other godly
learned men; notwithstanding our hand-writing which is in our
hands, no man (except God alone) can make it common, nor
any unworthy person is able to bereave us of it. But we shall
help with secret aid this so good a cause, as God shal permit or
hinder us: For our God is not blinde, as the Heathens *Fortuna*,
but is the Churches Ornament, and the honor of the Temple.
Our *Philosophy* also is not a new Invention, but as *Adam* after

his *fall* hath received it, and as *Moses* and *Solomon* used it; also she ought not much to be doubted of, or contradicted by other opinions, or meanings; but seeing the truth is peaceable, brief, and always like her self in all things, and especially accorded by with *Jesus in omni parte* and all members. And as he is the true Image of the Father, so is she his Image; It shal not be said, this is true according to *Philosophy*, but true according to *Theologie*; And wherein *Plato, Aristotle, Pythagoras* and others did hit the mark, and wherein *Enoch, Abraham, Moses, Solomon* did excel; but especially wherewith that wonderful book the *Bible* agreeth. All that same concurreth together, and make a Sphere or Globe, whose total parts are equidistant from the Center, as hereof more at large and more plain shal be spoken of in Christianly Conference.

But now concerning (and chiefly in this our age) the ungodly and accursed *Gold-making*, which hath gotten so much the upper hand, whereby under colour of it, many runagates and roguish people do use great villanies, and cozen and abuse the credit which is given them: yea nowadays men of discretion do hold the transmutation of Mettals to be the highest point, and *fastigium* in *Philosophy*, this is all their intent, and desire, and that God would be most esteemed by them, and honored, which could make great store of Gold, and in abundance, the which with unpremeditate prayers, they hope to attain of the alknowing God, and searchers of all hearts: we therefore do by these presents publickly testifie, that the true *Philosophers* are far of another minde, esteeming little the making of Gold, which is but a *parergon*; for besides that they have a thousand better things.

And we say with our loving *Father R. C. C. Phy: aurum nisi quantum aurum*, for unto them the whole nature is detected: he doth not rejoyce, that he can make Gold, and that, as saith Christ, the devils are obedient unto him; but is glad that he seeth the Heavens open, and the Angels of God ascending and descending, and his name written in the book of life. Also we do testifie that under the name of *Chymia* many books and pictures are set forth in *Contumeliam gloria Dei*, as we wil name them in their due season, and wil give to the pure-hearted a Catalogue, or Register of them: And we pray all learned men to take heed of these kinde of Books; for the enemy never resteth, but soweth his weeds, til a stronger one doth root it out. So according to the wil and meaning of *Fra: C. R. C.* we his brethren request again all the learned in *Europe*, who shal read (sent forth in five Languages) this our *Famam* and *Confessionem*, that it would please them with good deliberation to ponder this our offer, and to examine most nearly and most sharply their Arts, and behold the present time with all diligence, and to declare their minde, either *Communicato consilio*, or *singulatim* by Print.

And although at this time we make no mention either of our names, or meetings, yet nevertheless every ones opinion shal assuredly come to our hands, in what language so ever it be; nor any body shal fail, who so gives but his name to speak with some of us, either by word of mouth, or else if there be some lett in writing. And this we say for a truth, That whosoever shal earnestly, and from his heart, bear affection unto us, it shal be beneficial to him in goods, body and soul; but he that is false-hearted, or onely greedy of riches, the same first of all shal not be able in any manner of wise to hurt us, but bring himself to utter ruine and destruction. Also our building (although one hundred thousand people had very near seen and beheld the same) shal for ever remain untouched, undestroyed, and hidden to the wicked world, *sub umbra alarum tuarum Jehova.*[17]

From: *A Christian Rosenkreutz Anthology*, compiled and edited by Paul M. Allen in collaboration with Carlo Pietzner. Editorial and reference notes by Paul M. Allen. Published by Rudolf Steiner Publications, a division of Garber Communications, 1981. Archive edition, Great Barrington, MA 2000.

Notes

References from the works of Rudolf Steiner given in the following notes refer to the pages of the German editions (GA). Passages have been newly translated to give consistency of terminology.

1   GA 99, p. 14 and GA 264, p. 327.
2   GA 98, p. 16.
3   Cf. Rudolf Steiner: *Anthroposophie und Rosenkreuzertum. Ausgewählte Texte.* Edited by Andreas Neider. Dornach 2007. The first important collection of Rudolf Steiner's references to the Rosicrucians was published and introduced by the anthroposophist and astrologer Paul Regenstreif (1899-1981): *Christian Rosenkreutz und seine Mission. Als Studienmaterial auf der Grundlage von Hinweisen Rudolf Steiners zusammengestellt und bearbeitet von Paul Regenstreif.* Freiburg 1977. Since Steiner's collected works in German (GA) have by now been almost completely edited and published, Neider's more recent publication is more comprehensive. The quality and composition of this work are impressive and it contains a concise commentary. Regenstreif's work is nonetheless remarkable in its focus on essential aspects. He began his introduction with the words: "What Rudolf Steiner wanted to tell us about Christian Rosenkreutz forms a unique part of his life work. The only coherent presentations were given in the years 1911/1912. I will try to present references that will help the reader to study the individuality of Christian Rosenkreutz, or one could say: to come closer to his essence!" (p. 5).
4   GA 141, p. 91.
5   GA 130, p. 57.
6   Cf. the destiny of Rudolf Steiner's confidential presentations about the "Fifth Gospel" in: Peter Selg: *Rudolf Steiner und die Vorträge über das Fünfte Evangelium.* Dornach 2010,

p. 134. In English: *Rudolf Steiner and the Fifth Gospel*. Tr. Catherine E. Creeger. SteinerBooks 2010.

7   Paul Regenstreif: *Christian Rosenkreuz und seine Mission*, p. 25.

8   GA 98, p. 44.

9   Ibid., p. 16.

10   GA 133, p. 162.

11   GA 130, p. 322.

12   GA 133, p. 170.

13   GA 265, p. 435.

14   GA 130, p. 157.

15   GA 133, p. 21f.

16   GA 130, p. 311.

17   John 1:5.

18   GA 133, p. 162.

19   This is why the names of those who "received the [Rosicrucian] inspiration" remained unknown throughout the centuries, or they were only known to initiates, as Rudolf Steiner pointed out in Neuchâtel on September 27, 1911.

20   Ibid., p. 335.

21   Ibid.

22   Ibid., p. 313.

23   Cf. Hella Wiesberger: "Aus der okkulten Geschichtsforschung: Die Hiram – Johannes Individualität." In: Hella Wiesberger: *Rudolf Steiners esoterische Lehrtätigkeit*. Dornach 1997, p. 251-267 and Hella Krause Zimmer: *Christian Rosenkreutz. Die Inkarnationen*. Dornach 2009. According to Hella Wiesberger's detailed descriptions Rudolf Steiner first spoke about Lazarus-John in winter 1901/02 (Wiesberger, loc. cit., p. 251f.). Steiner mentioned Christian Rosenkreutz's reincarnation as Count St. Germain for the first time on November 11, 1904, in Berlin (GA 93), where he also referred indirectly to a connection with Hiram Abiff. Steiner probably spoke about Hiram's reincarnation as Lazarus-John for the first time in his esoteric school at Easter 1908, almost a year after the Munich Congress. Christian Rosenkreutz's destinies in the thirteenth, fourteenth, and fifteenth centuries were the

subject of his lectures in Neuchâtel on September 27 and 28, 1911 (GA 130). Steiner never spoke about the direct connection between the incarnations of Lazarus-John and Christian Rosenkreutz in lectures, only in private conversations, most probably for the first time shortly after the Neuchâtel lectures. "We find a certain evidence for this assumption in the triptych 'Grail' that was, according to Marie Steiner, painted shortly after the Neuchâtel lectures by artist Anna May. Its central panel shows the event of Golgotha, with Joseph of Arimathea collecting Christ's blood; the left panel depicts figures from the Temple Legend: King Solomon, the Queen of Sheba, and Hiram Abiff; the right panel shows Christian Rosenkreutz's initiation in the thirteenth century, which was first described by Rudolf Steiner in Neuchâtel. Rudolf Steiner is said to have given Anna May the relevant indications." (Wiesberger, loc. cit., p. 258). According to Margarethe Hauschka, who is Anna May's niece, the "Triptych Grail" was originally painted for the Johannes building in Munich, later for the first Goetheanum where Anna May worked on the stained glass windows for a time. Her comprehensive painting—Hauschka estimated its size at 13 x 8 feet—was exhibited publicly in Munich in 1918 in the art gallery Das Reich that Alexander von Bernus had opened in November 1917 in the Königinstrasse, and in the Glass Palace. For the Exhibition in the Glass Palace, Anna May wrote a description of the painting titled: "From Solomon through Golgotha to Christian Rosenkreutz." There she wrote: "The Mystery of Golgotha is the crucial event in human history. 'Grail' is the word for the human being who seeks access to that event. Legend has it that the grail was carved from the stone that dropped out of Lucifer's crown when he fell. Solomon received it from the Queen of Sheba (left panel of the triptych). It then becomes the chalice of the Last Supper that Joseph of Arimathea used to collect the blood (center panel). Once the blood of Christ will have penetrated to the innermost depths of the earth in the distant future, the whole Christ-permeated human being, the Parzival of the future, will awaken from the grail chalice and rise as out of a coffin to unite all religions and earlier philosophies within the living Christ-knowledge. By then Michael will have bound the dragon and the 'woman' of the apocalypse will again carry the sun within her and the moon under her feet. That means that the earth will have conquered matter. The upper part of the triptych 'Grail' represents the spiritual world (gold); the uppermost larger heads are the spirits of time (archai) that hold hands through the ages, and alternate. They are supported by the folk spirits (archangels). Below those are the angeloi or angels who look down on humanity. The lower part, the two columns, represents the blood stream that flows through humanity. In connection with the spiritual (gold), it incarnates the sublime leaders of human evolution." (Quoted from Margarethe Hauschka: "Das Triptychon 'Gral' von Anna May." In: Das Goetheanum, no. 24, 1974.) In this text, which was meant for the public, Anna May did not refer to Christian Rosenkreutz and his initiation in the thirteenth century that is impressively depicted on the right side panel of the triptych. The exhibition in the art gallery Das Reich and in the Glass Palace took place around the time of Steiner's comments on the Chymical Wedding (cf. p. 70ff.). The triptych had been kept at the Hamburg Waldorf School, but it was destroyed by bombs in World War II.

24   This relationship was misunderstood and distorted by Gerhard Wehrs, among others, in his contribution at the Symposium "Rosenkreuz as a European Phenomenon of the 17th Century," organized in 1994 by the Herzog August Bibliothek in Wolfenbüttel and the Bibliotheka Philosophica Hermetica in Amsterdam. Wehr spoke about "Rosicrucianism in Rudolf Steiner's work," referring to "Steiner's abstruse constructions." (In: Rosenkreuz als europäisches Phänomen im 17. Jahrhundert. Ed. Bibliotheca Philosophica Hermetic. Amsterdam 2002, p. 361-378).

25   Friedrich Rittelmeyer, Meine Lebensbegegnung mit Rudolf Steiner: Stuttgart 1983, p. 102f. In English: Rudolf Steiner Enters My Life. Tr. D. S. Osmond. Floris Books.

26 Perseus Verlag Basel, Archives. See Peter Selg: *Rudolf Steiner und Felix Koguzki. Der Beitrag des Kräutersammlers zur Anthroposophie.* Arlesheim 2008, p. 109/119. Friedrich Rittelmeyer discussed these matters also with Michael Bauer, as Margareta Morgenstern informed Emil Bock in a written note: "R. Steiner had said to Rittelm. that Master Jesus had referred him to Fichte." (Note from Margareta Morgenstern for Emil Bock. Quoted from Klaus J. Bracker: *Grals Initiation. Anthroposophische Esoterik und die künftige Jesus-Offenbarung.* Stuttgart 2009, p. 170).

27 See Peter Selg: *Rudolf Steiner und Felix Koguzki. Der Beitrag des Kräutersammlers zur Anthroposophie,* p. 114ff.

28 Rudolf Steiner said in an autobiographical lecture of February 4, 1913, that his esoteric training had taken place after his meeting with Felix through a personality "using a tool to inspire in the boy, who was standing in the spiritual world, the regular, systematic knowledge needed in the spiritual world. The personality used ... the works of Fichte. On their basis, certain considerations could arise that held the seeds for the spiritual science that the man whom the boy grew up to be, wrote down. Much of what later appeared in *Occult Science* was considered then in connection with Fichte's writings." (In: Rudolf Steiner: *Selbstzeugnisse. Autobiographische Dokumente.* Dornach 2009, p. 46f.) Rudolf Steiner referred to that personality as a 'master' and made notes for Schuré in 1907 about his encounter with him (and the preceding meeting with Felix Koguzki): "I did not meet the M. [Master] immediately but someone sent by him who was fully initiated into the secrets of all plants, how they worked and how they related to the cosmos and to human nature" (ibid., p. 88). See also following note.

29 Walter Johannes Stein said in a lecture: "Schuré asked Rudolf Steiner who had initiated him and the answer was Master Jesus. Schuré confirmed this on his deathbed." (Quoted from Klaus J. Bracker: *Grals Initiation. Anthroposophische Esoterik und die künftige Jesus-Offenbarung.* Stuttgart 2009, p. 168; for the Fichte context see ibid., p. 177ff.).

30 For "Master Jesus" see in particular GA 114 (lecture of September 21, 1909) and GA 264.
31 See Peter Selg: *Rudolf Steiner und Felix Koguzki. Der Beitrag des Kräutersammlers zur Anthroposophie*, p. 114ff.
32 GA 28, p. 60.
33 GA 44, p. 211.
34 For this concept see Hella Wiesberger: "Aus der okkulten Geschichtsforschung: Die Lehre von den großen Geistesführern der Menschheit." In: *Rudolf Steiners esoterische Lehrtätigkeit*, p. 73ff.
35 GA 129, p. 152ff.
36 GA 262, p. 16.
37 See in particular the copious quotations from Koguzki's diary in "Zur Geschichte und Lebenswelt Felix Koguzkis." In: Peter Selg: *Rudolf Steiner und Felix Koguzki. Der Beitrag des Kräutersammlers zur Anthroposophie*, p. 31-51.
38 GA 130, p. 274; emphasis added.
39 Ibid., p. 273.
40 GA 264, p. 87.
41 See GA 26, p. 143ff. Rudolf Steiner wrote there about the preparatory work of the Rosicrucians: "Some individualities, who understood the position of Michael's forces in the cosmos, strove to prepare their soul forces for conscious access to the spirit realm that borders the earthly realm, where Michael works for humankind. They sought to acquire eligibility for this spiritual endeavor by behaving in their professional lives, and otherwise, in a way that made it impossible to distinguish their lives from that of other people. Because they fulfilled their earthly duties out of love, in an ordinary way, they could devote themselves inwardly, freely to the spiritual. Their inner life was wholly their own concern and that of those with whom they connected "secretly." At first the world seemed untouched physically by this spiritual striving. Yet, it was all essential to create the necessary connection of human souls with the world of Michael. They were not "secret societies" in a negative sense. They did not seek the occult because they feared the light of day. They

found each other and ensured that those who joined them were conscious of the Michael mission in the right way. Those who work together in this way do not speak of their work to others who might disturb their tasks through lack of understanding. These tasks are related to spiritual streams that do not belong to the earth, but to the adjacent spirit world from which they send impulses to the earth. It is the spiritual work of individuals who live in the physical world but work together with beings of the spiritual world, with beings who do not enter the physical world, who do not incarnate. It is the work of what the world refers to (often incorrectly) as the "Rosicrucians." True Rosicrucianism is indeed related to Michael's mission. It helped Michael to prepare on earth his spiritual work that was intended for a future age."

42 Rudolf Steiner spoke about Goethe's relationship to Rosicrucianism in many lectures—in connection with *Faust*, the poem "The Mysteries," and the *"Tale of the Green Snake and the Beautiful Lily"*—and his literary work in general ("Goethe's greatest poetic deeds are rooted in Rosicrucianism" GA 57, p. 440). According to Hella Wiesberger, Steiner wrote a short text about this in 1906 for Edouard Schuré, "Goethe and his relationship to Rosicrucianism." A handwritten copy of this text by Marie Steiner-von Sivers has been preserved, and was published in GA 93: "There are two ways of penetrating Goethe's Rosicrucian mystery: an exoteric and an esoteric or occult way. The esoteric path is revealed through a study of those of Goethe's poems that are an outward expression of his Rosicrucian views and other knowledge relevant to this question. These include: 1) The poem "The Mysteries." It describes the mystery of the lodge of the twelve, with the thirteenth at their head. The contents are a reference to the experiences in the outer court of the Rosicrucian Parzival initiation (Grail initiation). 2) The basic theme of *Faust*. Homunculus is the astral body; the journey to the "Mothers" is a representation of the search for the Golden Triangle and the Lost Word. 3) The passages in *Wilhelm Meister* portraying the "Journey and Transformation of the

Soul" as far as the extension of consciousness to cosmic vision (Contemplation of cosmic events. Makarios' vision is such an act of contemplation.). 4) *The Tale of the Green Snake and the Beautiful Lily* is a portrayal of an *alchemical initiation* as established by Christian Rosenkreutz: this is written correctly (not as in the defective tradition of the Lodges) as 030 degree (commonly known in Freemasonry parlance as the 30th degree). This fable contains in symbolic language all the secrets, just as the myth of Hercules contains all the secrets of the Royal Arch degree, which is properly written 013 degree and which is also called the fourth degree. 5) Important aspects of Rosicrucian initiation are also to be found in the poem "Pandora."

The means of penetrating Goethe's Rosicrucianism in an esoteric or occult way are given in the initiation of the true 020 degree, which (to conceal the secret) is also written as 6 3 degree being read as 6 x 3 = 18th degree (Rose-Croix). In this it is shown, in an occult way, that Goethe underwent an initiation between his visits to Leipzig and Strasbourg, which came to fruition in his life only gradually, and which enabled him to fulfill a very particular Rosicrucian mission. No more about this can be *written down*: one could still say a little more about it verbally; and still more only in a *true* Rosicrucian Lodge of the 6 3 = 6 x 3 = 18th degree" (GA 93, p. 291f.). For Goethe's initiation, which only gradually "came to fruition" in his life, see note 224.

43   GA 114, p. 137.
44   Ibid.
45   See Rudolf Steiner: "Theosophie in Deutschland vor 100 Jahren." Lecture given in Paris on June 4, 1906. In: GA 35, p. 43-65.
46   GA 28, p. 365f.
47   Ibid., p. 394.
48   Rudolf Steiner: *Selbstzeugnisse. Autobiographische Dokumente*, p. 90f.
49   "When Christian Rosenkreutz brought Eastern wisdom to Europe, he founded schools where the students were brought

up to levels that allowed them to see into Devachan, to see the higher mysteries. Only the initiated can speak of this. Outer forms, all the knowledge of books, cannot teach them anything. Up to the year 1875, when the Theosophical Society was founded, these matters were not spoken of anywhere but in the most secret schools. Only from 1875 have the Masters of Wisdom felt that they had to convey something of these profound spiritual truths to humanity," Rudolf Steiner said in Berlin on February 25, 1904 (GA 88, p. 134f.). Three and a half years later, in autumn 1907, he wrote down for Edouard Schuré that the foundation of the Theosophical Society in 1875 "had had a truly Western character." He added that the "great initiates of the West" were also the "initiators of Rosicrucian wisdom" (GA 262, p. 24. For Rudolf Steiner's concept of the "West," see Hella Wiesberger: "Central Europe is, globally speaking, part of the Western world. Rudolf Steiner therefore referred to the two Masters of the West [Christian Rosenkreutz and Master Jesus] as the ones who were important for Central Europe." (Hella Wiesberger: "Aus der okkulten Geschichtsforschung: Die Lehre von den großen Geistesführern der Menschheit." In: *Rudolf Steiners esoterische Lehrtätigkeit*, p. 80). Rudolf Steiner pointed out repeatedly that Helena Petrovna Blavatsky's first writings (the spiritual center of the early Theosophical Society) had been inspired by Rosicrucianism. On January 27, 1912, he said in Cassel: "... The first writings of the founder of the Theosophical Society, the great personality H.P. Blavatsky, can only be explained on the basis of their underlying Rosicrucian inspiration" (GA 130, p. 233). This applied particularly to the two volumes of *Isis Unveiled*, published in New York in 1877, two years after the Theosophical Society had been founded there. In Neuchâtel, Rudolf Steiner said on September 27, 1911 (GA 130, p. 67) that *Isis Unveiled* had been inspired by the "emanations" of Christian Rosenkreutz' etheric body. See also the remarkable lectures of "The Transcendental Universe," given by the English esotericist C.F. Harrison in London early in

1893. (Available as: *The Transcendental Universe: Six lectures on Occult Science, Theosophy, and the Catholic Faith.* Introduction by Christopher Bamford. Great Barrington, MA: Lindisfarne Books 1993).

50   Rudolf Steiner's letter to Marie von Sivers of January 9, 1905 (GA 262, p. 86).

51   GA 264, p. 243.

52   GA 34, p. 537.

53   GA 52, p. 282.

54   GA 93, p. 58f.

55   GA 264, p. 281.

56   GA 94, p. 176; emphasis added.

57   GA 264, p. 280.

58   GA 55, p. 178.

59   Ibid., p. 181.

60   Ibid., p. 182.

61   GA 264, p. 282f; emphasis added.

62   GA 55, p. 177; emphasis added.

63   Ibid., p. 176.

64   GA 158, p. 201.

65   Instead of "I[n] J[esu] M[orimur] Rudolf Steiner wrote "I[n] C[hristo] M[orimur]" and added "Sanctum" in "P[er] S[piritum] S[anctum] R[eviviscimus]." He wore a rose cross around his neck that still bore the old initials: EDN, IJM, PSSR (see p. 2).

66   GA 284, p. 43ff.

67   The lecture cycle was puublished as *Die Theosophie des Rosenkreutzers.* In English: *Rosicrucian Wisdom.* Tr. J. Collis. Forest Row, U.K.: Rudolf Steiner Press 2000.

68   GA 264, p. 280.

69   GA 99, p. 12.

70   Ibid., p. 14.

71   Ibid., p. 14.

72   See "Tode im Denken. Zur Entwicklung des Materialismus im 19. Jahrhundert." In: Peter Selg: *Michael und Christus. Studien zur Anthroposophie Rudolf Steiners.* Arlesheim 2010, p. 241–262. Rudolf Steiner's indications regarding the

withdrawal of the Rosicrucian impulses (and of Christian Rosenkreutz himself) in the nineteenth century might be connected with his comments on Goethe's partial spiritual failing after Schiller's death. (See Peter Selg: *Friedrich Schiller. Die Geistigkeit des Willens.* Dornach 2005, p. 198ff.) Goethe's resigned attitude to the technological developments, which he expressed in his letter to Carl Friedrich Zelter of June 6, 1885, might also be connected with this (temporarily) interrupted process: "Wealth and rapidity are what the world admires, and what everyone strives to attain. Railways, quick mails, steamships, and every possible kind of facility in the way of communication are what the educated world has in view, that it may over-educate itself, and thereby continue in a state of mediocrity.... Properly speaking, this is the century for clever people, for practical people of quick perception, who, because they possess a certain adroitness, feel their superiority to the multitude, even though they themselves may not be gifted in the highest degree. Let us, as far as possible, keep the attitude with which we came here; we shall, with a few others, be the last of an era that will not so soon return again" (Ibid., p. 96). English translation adapted from www.ebooksread.com/authors-eng/johann-wolfgang-von-goethe/goethes-letters-to-zelter-with-extracts-from-those-of-zelter-to-goethe-hci/page-20-goethes-letters-to-zelter-with-extracts-from-those-of-zelter-to-goethe-hci.shtml, accessed July 27, 2011.

73   "The doctor also said that if he could have continued his work in Paris consistently, after he was there once in 1906, there would not have been a war. I cannot forget words of that kind, and we must take them seriously" (Ita Wegman: Letter to Eugen Kolisko, May 2, 1928. Ita Wegman Archives, Arlesheim). "At the time [in May 1924] he said the crucial words to me: 'If it had been possible to establish an anthroposophic center in Paris, war would not have broken out in 1914...'" (Ita Wegman: Letter to Albert Steffen, May 24, 1928. Ita Wegman Archives, Arlesheim). Rudolf Steiner first visited Paris in May/June 1906. He gave a course of cosmological lectures and participated in the third congress of the

Theosophical Society's Federation of European Sections. There it was decided that the next congress would take place in Germany. Steiner then prepared the great Rosicrucian initiative of 1907 in Munich. His words to Ita Wegman must be seen against this background.

74 GA 99, p. 17f.

75 GA 109, p. 161.

76 See Hella Wiesberger: "Die Trennung der 'Esoteric School of Theosophy' und der 'Theosophical Society'" in *Rudolf Steiners esoterische Lehrtätigkeit*, p. 133-156.

77 Sergei O. Prokofieff wrote that the Western masters Christian Rosenkreutz and Master Jesus, "through their delegate Rudolf Steiner," ruled out a continued membership in the school of the Eastern masters for their pupils. Prokofieff pointed out: "In the overall context of the esoteric lesson (the first after the official separation of the two esoteric schools) this interdiction could only be a direct confirmation of the separation within the circle of the masters themselves. The emergence of two independent esoteric schools and of two independent societies five years later could consequently only be the earthly reflection of that separation." (*Die Geburt der christlichen Esoterik im 20. Jahrhundert und die ihr widerstrebenden Mächte*. Dornach 1997, p. 29. In English as *The East in the Light of the West*. Parts 1-3. Forest Row, U.K.: Temple Lodge 2010).

78 GA 264, p. 329f.

79 Ibid., p. 331f.

80 Concerning Rudolf Steiner's esoteric lessons after the Munich separation, Sergei O. Prokofieff has written: "Immediately after the final separation of the Western esoteric school from the Eastern school, Rudolf Steiner began (as if relieved from a burden) to reveal with unprecedented intensity and depth Christian esoteric wisdom. In the esoteric lessons (of which he gave several hundred up to the beginning of World War I) the Eastern mahatmas were no longer mentioned. They were replaced henceforth by the inspirations and the suprasensory presence of the Western masters, the great teachers of

Rosicrucianism. In each lesson Rudolf Steiner looked at new aspects of Christian esotericism. The three Rosicrucian mottoes, which express the true essence of the Christ Mystery, have a central place in most lessons." (*Die Geburt der christlichen Esoterik im 20. Jahrhundert und die ihr widerstrebenden Mächte*, p. 41f. In English: *The East in the Light of the West*. Parts 1-3).

81 GA 262, p. 26.
82 GA 118, p. 28.
83 See GA 118.
84 GA 262, p. 23.
85 Rudolf Steiner, quoted from Marie Savitch: *Marie Steiner-von Sivers. Mitarbeiterin Rudolf Steiners*. Dornach 1965, p. 84. Alexander Strakosch wrote in his memoirs of Rudolf Steiner, with reference to the Krishnamurti affair: "...it was deeply painful to see how Rudolf Steiner suffered from these signs of decay in the Theosophical Society. He did not usually speak of himself; but once, when it was really bad, he said quietly: 'This matter will cost me five years of my life.'" (*Lebenswege mit Rudolf Steiner. Erinnerungen*. Dornach 1994, p. 75).
86 GA 266a, p. 251.
87 GA 98, p. 45.
88 "Within this whole stream, the initiation of Mani, who initiated Christian Rosenkreutz in 1459, is seen as a 'higher degree.' It consists of the true insight into the mission of evil. This initiation with its background will have to be kept concealed from the public for a long time" (GA 262, p. 24). Just a week after his first comprehensive lecture on the Rosicrucians in Berlin ("The Mystery of the Rosicrucians," November 4, 1904), Steiner spoke about Manichaeism there (November 11, 1904). In an esoteric lesson, Rudolf Steiner said about Mani, the founder of Manichaeism, the reincarnated Youth of Nain, whom Christ had once raised from the dead (GA 264, p. 228f.): "His teachings included all the wisdom of the ancient religions, which he illuminated with a Christian gnosis so that the believers in Babylonian-Egyptian star wisdom, the followers of the ancient Persian religion,

and even the Buddhists from India could be penetrated by an understanding of the Christ impulse. The soul of Mani, which had lived in the Youth of Nain, and which had been initiated by Christ for the future, prepared the time when everything contained in Manichaeism that has not been fully unfolded yet, would rise up for the salvation of the ancient Eastern peoples. When this soul was incarnated as Mani, it prepared its real later mission: the uniting in harmony of all religions" (ibid., p. 229f.). On August 31, 1909 (GA 113), Rudolf Steiner spoke in Munich about Mani's central importance for the Rosicrucian stream (the Christ-permeated harmony of all religions). He described a crucial event that took place in the *fourth century A.D.* in the form of a spiritual "conference" under Mani's direction: "At the conference a plan was established for all the wisdom of the bodhisattvas of the post-Atlantean era to flow more and more intensely into the future of humanity. The plan established then for the future cultural development of the earth was preserved, and flowed into the European mysteries of the Rosy Cross" (GA 113, p. 192). All four members of that conference (Mani, Buddha, Skythianos, and Zarathustra or Master Jesus) would later, after the foundation of Rosicrucianism in the thirteenth and fourteenth centuries, be teachers "in the schools of the Rosy Cross"; "... teachers who send their wisdom to the earth as a gift that would make it possible to comprehend the true Christ" (ibid.).

This means that the occult Rosicrucian movement was prepared nine centuries before it was established on earth, exactly in the middle of the fourth post-Atlantean era, at a time when the last remnants of the ancient mysteries were lost forever. Under the direction of Mani, the four individualities planned and established a spiritual movement that would receive the content of the ancient mysteries in a new, Christ-imbued form, so that could be carried over into the future. According to Rudolf Steiner, Mani lived as Parzival in the ninth century, as the bearer of the Grail stream, which was, as Steiner pointed out repeatedly, related to the later

Rosicrucian movement. ("From the thirteenth and fourteenth centuries, Rosicrucianism has educated the initiates who are the successors of the ancient European mysteries and of the School of the Holy Grail" (GA 57, p. 439; "The task of cultivating Christian initiation was assigned to those who cultivated the Holy Grail; and later for the community of the Rosy Cross." GA 143, p. 149). The Mani individuality in its Parzival incarnation had sought the East (as Rosenkreutz would do later) for the sake of uniting the religions of the Eastern and Western streams of mystery wisdom; preparing itself for its task as "a new teacher of Christianity"; "… whose mission it will be to penetrate Christianity more and more with the teachings of karma and reincarnation when the time is ripe for this" (GA 264, p. 230).

89 GA 98, p. 45.

90 GA 99, p. 14.

91 GA 98, p. 45.

92 Ibid.

93 GA 109, p. 159.

94 GA 266a, p. 219.

95 See note 88.

96 On the great cosmological-Christological cycles of the year 1909 see my study: *Christian Morgenstern. Sein Weg mit Rudolf Steiner.* Stuttgart 2008, p. 55-145.

97 GA 14.

98 "The reason for the cancellation was obvious: A. Besant had planned to present Krishnamurti personally to the members of the congress as the new Messiah and head of the order 'Star of the East,' while Steiner wanted to give a lecture on the true relationship of the Christ being to Gautama Buddha and the Maitreya Buddha, which was to culminate in an in-depth description of the bodhisattva sphere in relation to the Christ." (Sergei O. Prokofieff: *Die Geburt der christlichen Esoterik im 20. Jahrhundert und die ihr widerstrebenden Mächte.* Dornach 1997, p. 103. In English: *The East in the Light of the West.* Parts 1-3.

99 GA 130, p. 57.

100 GA 133, p. 22.

101 See the lectures given in Munich (November 20, 1911, Stuttgart (November 28, 1911), Cassel (January 27 and 29), Vienna (February 9, 1912), and Hamburg (June 17, 1912); all in GA 130. Some aspects of these lectures and additional considerations would later flow into the theme of the Neuchâtel lectures.

102 For the inner relationship between Rudolf Steiner and Paracelsus (and the occult relationship between Goethe and Paracelsus) see Peter Selg: "Rudolf Steiner and Paracelsus" in: Peter Selg: *Michael und Christus. Studien zur Anthroposophie Rudolf Steiners*. Arlesheim 2010, p. 113-134.

103 Regarding the significance of the year 1250 for the spiritual development of humanity, see especially GA 15, p. 58ff., where Steiner wrote: "With the approach of the year 1250, a new spiritual guidance to spiritual worlds began. This guidance was prepared by the spirits who stood behind the external historical events of that time. Centuries before, they had prepared what would be needed for esoteric training under the conditions that prevailed in 1250. If the term "modern esotericism" is not abused, it can be applied to the spiritual work of these advanced individualities. Outer history has no recognition of them, although their activities became manifest throughout the entire culture that has evolved in the West since the thirteenth century. The significance of the year 1250 for the spiritual development of humanity becomes especially apparent when one considers the following results from clairvoyant research. Even individualities who had achieved very high levels of development in former incarnations and reincarnated around the year 1250 had to experience the total obliteration of their immediate insight into the spiritual world. The most enlightened individuals seemed as though cut off from the spiritual world, and could know of it only from their memory of earlier incarnations. This shows that a new element had to enter the spiritual guidance of humanity from that time. It was the element of true modern esotericism. Only with this element is it

possible to understand how the Christ impulse can flow into the guidance of all humanityand of individual human beings and their actions.

Between the Mystery of Golgotha and the arrival of modern esotericism lies the period when human souls first received the Christ principle. They received the Christ unconsciously for their higher spiritual faculties; later, when they were forced to receive it consciously, they made all sorts of mistakes, and confusion arose as to how the Christ was to be understood. It is possible to observe how in early Christianity the Christ principle lived itself into subordinated soul forces. Then a new period began, in which we still live today. In certain respects our understanding of what the Christ principle means for the higher soul faculties is still underdeveloped. It will be shown in what follows that the decline in suprasensory insight up to the thirteenth century, and its gradual reawakening in a different form since then, coincide with the intervention of the Christ impulse in human evolution. Modern esotericism can therefore be seen as the raising of the Christ impulse to a position where it can be the driving force of the souls who are ready to strive for knowledge of the higher worlds in a way that is suitable for modern times" (ibid.). Rudolf Steiner wrote these thoughts down in *August 1911*, a few weeks before he gave the Neuchâtel lectures, and published them in the book *The Spiritual Guidance of the Individual and Humanity* (GA 15), which was based on lectures he had given in Copenhagen in June 1911.

For the astronomical-cosmological dimension of the year of change—1250—a "nodal point" and "deep incision" in the history of humanity, see especially Rudolf Steiner's descriptions of December 31, 1910, and January 1, 1911, in Stuttgart (GA 126), nine months before Neuchâtel. See also Paul Regenstreif, who wrote about the time of Christian Rosenkreutz' initiation in the middle of the thirteenth century: "The event is related to a unique star constellation that is not characterized by a rhythm in the planetary spheres, but by occurrences in the sphere of the fixed stars, which also explains the duration of what has been described. Rudolf Steiner referred to what occurred around 1248 under various aspects; for instance, in Copenhagen on June 7, 1911 (GA 15); in Stuttgart on December 31, 1910, and January 1, 1911 (GA 126); and on January 6, 1921 (GA 203). Rudolf Steiner became interested in these rhythms at an early age. During his schooling in Vienna-Neustadt in the years 1875–1878 he had a teacher, Dr. Franz Kofler, who wrote a school essay in which Steiner was so interested that he remembered it in his autobiography. 'The history and geography teacher who gave me so little in the lower classes, nevertheless became important for me once I was in the upper classes. The very teacher who had driven me to study Kant in such a peculiar way, wrote an essay for the curriculum: "The Ice Age and Its Causes." I read it eagerly, and retained a lively interest in the problem of the Ice Age.' [English translation of this quote taken from: Rudolf Steiner: *Autobiography* (GA 28), p. 23, tr. R. Stebbing.] Ten years later, in 1889, Rudolf Steiner himself wrote an article on the Ice Age problem for an encyclopedia (*Pierers Konversationslexikon*). The star constellation of the thirteenth century mentioned earlier has indeed a connection with the Ice Age chronology, a rhythm of c. 21,000 years caused by the precession movement (25,920 years), and the movement of the apsides (c. 110,000 years). The points of the winter solstice and perihelion (closest to the sun) met, and [the initiation of Christian Rosenkreutz] took place on earth in 1248." (Paul Regenstreif: *Christian Rosenkreutz und seine Mission*, p. 13f.).

104 GA 130, p. 60; see also GA 130, p. 229 and p. 266.
105 GA 130, p. 155.
106 See also GA 151.
107 GA 130, p. 62.
108 See note 88.
109 GA 130, p. 230.
110 Ibid., p. 268.
111 See Hella Krause-Zimmer: *Christian Rosenkreutz. Die Inkarnationen*. Dornach 2009.

112 GA 130, p. 61.

113 See note 88.

114 GA 130, p. 155.

115 Ibid., p. 268.

116 See note 131.

117 GA 130, p. 62.

118 Ibid., p. 269.

119 Ibid., p. 270. Rudolf Steiner said in Neuchâtel that the education of spirit and soul worked right into the physiology *because* the child had such a weak constitution: "He was a very delicate child in that incarnation of the thirteenth century; that is why the education of the twelve worked into his physical body" (ibid., p. 62, emphasis added).

120 Ibid.

121 According to Rudolf Steiner's description of February 2, 1912, in Vienna, the fact that the body "became transparent" was not directly related to the fact that he did not take in any food. He said at the time: "And remarkably, the greater and more harmonious the soul content of the boy grew, the more delicate his body became; more and more delicate. At a particular age the body had become so delicate that it was literally transparent, that one could see through his limbs. And the youth ate less and less, until in the end he stopped eating altogether." (GA 130, p. 270).

122 Ibid., p. 155.

123 Ibid., p. 63.

124 Ibid., p. 270.

125 Rudolf Steiner reported repeatedly that the twelve recorded these imaginations and worked through them. They became the "Secret Symbols of the Rosicrucians" that were published at the end of the eighteenth century. See Walter Schneider: *Die Lehren der Rosenkreuzer*. Stuttgart 2006.

126 GA 130, p. 63.

127 See note 88.

128 GA 130, p. 156.

129 Ibid., p. 63.

130 GA 109, p. 66.

131 Sergei O. Prokofieff wrote about the mid-thirteenth century initiation of Christian Rosenkreutz and the revitalization of his "transparent" body: "The process was so unique because, for the first time, a human physical body had been given new life through the powers of the phantom; and it received back the human "I" that had, just before, experienced the entire process described, observing it in full consciousness in the suprasensory world. Through this event, the foundation was laid in Earth evolution for the later possibility of human beings to absorb an imprint of the Christ-I into their individual "I"; of the "I" that the Christ had imprinted into the outer vessel of Jesus of Nazareth and that was afterward multiplied in the spiritual worlds according to the laws of spiritual economy." (*Die Grundsteinmeditation. Ein Schlüssel zu den neuen christlichen Mysterien.* Dornach 2003, p. 87. In English: *The Foundation Stone Mediation. A Key to the Christian Mysteries.* Tr. M. St. Goar. Forest Row, U.K.: Rudolf Steiner Press 2006).

132 GA 130, p. 63.

133 Ibid.

134 Ibid., p. 64.

135 Ibid., p. 232, emphasis added.

136 "During that time hardly anybody but the "Twelve" came to know Christian Rosenkreutz. That is not to say that he did not walk among people. It means that they did not recognize him" (ibid., p. 69). During the Christmas Conference of the General Anthroposophical Society 1923/1924, Rudolf Steiner spoke in detail about the meeting with Rosicrucian masters in the fourteenth and fifteenth centuries. On December 31, 1923, he said: "Those who aspired to true Rosicrucian instruction had to follow a path of esoteric spiritual development from the thirteenth or fourteenth centuries, and especially the fifteenth, for the Rosicrucian temples lay deeply hidden from exoteric physical experience. Many true Rosicrucians visited those temples, but no physical human eye ever beheld them. The old Rosicrucians, who were dispersed as hermits of wisdom and of sacred human acts, could,

however, be found by those able to perceive the divine in a mild, brilliant gaze. I am not referring to anything unreal. I am not describing a picture. I speak of a reality, which was of immense importance in the times to which I refer. Those who had acquired the faculty of reading the physical language of the heavens in the mild, brilliant gaze of someone's eyes were able to find the Rosicrucian master. They found these remarkable personalities whose souls were imbued with the divine, and who were inwardly connected with the spiritual temples. They found them in the most unassuming surroundings, under the most unassuming human conditions, especially in the fourteenth and fifteenth centuries in Central Europe. Finding the way to them was, however, as difficult as finding the way to the legendary Holy Grail." (GA 233, p.138).

137 GA 130, p. 76.

138 See in particular Rudolf Steiner's descriptions of September 28, 1911 in Neuchâtel. (GA 130).

139 GA 233a, p. 46.

140 GA 55, p. 182.

141 GA 233a, p. 46.

142 GA 266a, p. 251.

143 Ibid.

144 GA 130, p. 66f.

145 Ibid., p. 64.

146 GA 118. See also my study "Die Wiederkunft des Christus im Ätherischen" in: Peter Selg: *Michael und Christus. Studien zur Anthroposophie Rudolf Steiners*, p. 331–344. The "true harmony of all religions," which was mainly prepared and intended by Mani, and which inspired the initiation of Christian Rosenkreutz in the thirteenth century (driving him to his travels in the fourteenth/fifteenth centuries), is enhanced by the perception of the Christ in the etheric. Rudolf Steiner said in Neuchâtel: "From the twentieth century onward, all religions will be united in the Rosicrucian mystery. Such a union will be possible in the next three thousand years because there will no longer be any necessity to

teach humanity on the basis of texts. Human beings will learn to comprehend the Pauline event of Damascus because they will see the Christ. Humanity itself will go through the Pauline experience" (GA 130, p. 77f.).

147 "He is active not only through Christian Rosenkreutz, but also through all those who became his pupils" (GA 130, p. 66).

148 Ibid., p. 67f.

149 GA 117, p. 217; emphasis added.

150 See in particular Rudolf Steiner's lecture of November 9, 1914 (GA 258). For Christian Rosenkreutz' and Michael's joint preparation of the experience of the etheric Christ, see Sergei O. Prokofieff: *Die erste Klasse der Michael-Schule und ihre christologischen Grundlagen*. Dornach 2009, p. 390f.

151 GA 118, p. 28. Before the spiritual reappearance of the Christ can be experienced it is necessary, according to Rudolf Steiner, to spiritualize the experience of nature; "*first* we will have to come to a spiritual view of nature again." (GA 130, p. 77).

152 GA 130, p. 79.

153 Master Jesus was actively involved in the conception of the Rosicrucian movement in the fourth century (see note 88). Later he supported Christian Rosenkreutz, acting as a spiritual "teacher" (ibid.) in his school. Since the historical appearance of the Rosicrucian movement, which he had helped to prepare, he has been acting "in the spirit of Christian Rosenkreutz"; that is, he supports Christian Rosenkreutz in fulfilling his mission as the "leader of Western spiritual life." (GA 264, p. 238). Before the Rosicrucian movement assumed its activity, and during the preparation of that activity, Master Jesus had given the impulse for the Christian-mystical stream in Central Europe, which included the Dominican Johannes Tauler and Master Eckhart (and, indirectly, the religious-philosophical streams arising from them). Once Christian Rosenkreutz had begun to intervene in the occult history of the West, Master Jesus acted primarily in a supportive capacity. When Rudolf Steiner refers

to "Rosicrucian" impulses in his lectures (or to his own writings that were inspired by Rosicrucianism), we can assume an involvement of Master Jesus, even though Steiner did not mention him explicitly for reasons of discretion. Even when he used the singular (as in his letter to Marie von Sivers: "I can assure you: if the Master had not known how to persuade me, I would have continued to write philosophical books and speak about literature and philosophy *after* 1901, despite the need for theosophy in our age."), he might have referred to Christian Rosenkreutz as the only representative, but not necessarily as the only active influence. Although Christian Rosenkreutz is presently the "leader of Western spiritual life," we should not lose sight of the important role Master Jesus played in Rudolf Steiner's life and work, in the preparation and development of anthroposophy and its Christological orientation. There are other reasons for the fact that Steiner did not mention Master Jesus, who was his true master, according to Schuré (see notes 29 and 30); and there is no implication of inferiority to the position of Rosenkreutz. For particular aspects of Master Jesus' influence, see also Klaus J. Bracker: *Grals-Initiation. Anthroposophische Esoteric und die künftige Jesus-Offenbarung*. Stuttgart 2009.

154 GA 113, p. 194f.

155 GA 240, p. 18.

156 GA 268, p. 313.

157 October 1, 1911, in: GA 130. For Rudolf Steiner's presentation of the etherization of the blood in Basel, see Peter Selg: *Vom Logos menschlicher Physis. Die Entfaltung einer anthroposophischen Humanphysiologie im Werk Rudolf Steiners*. Vol. 1. Dornach 2006, p. 241ff. Having described the physiological background, Rudolf Steiner said, surprisingly, of its macrocosmic equivalent: "We have to describe the corresponding [macrocosmic] phenomenon today *as it has been revealed through the most meticulous esoteric research of the last years, undertaken in the spiritual investigations of individual true and genuine Rosicrucians*" (GA 130, p. 92; emphasis added). Steiner continued: "The blood

is continually transformed into etheric substance in the heart area, and a similar process takes place in the macrocosm. To understand this, we must look at the Mystery of Golgotha, and the moment when the blood flowed from the wounds of Christ Jesus. This blood is not to be seen merely as chemical substance; because of the nature of Jesus of Nazareth, which has been described, it is something entirely unique. When it flowed into the earth, a substance was imparted to the earth that, in uniting with it, constituted an event of the greatest importance for the future of the earth. It was an event that could take place only once. What happened with this blood in the times that followed? The same as happens with the blood in the human heart. In the course of earth evolution, this blood went through an etherization process. And as our blood flows as ether from the heart upward, the etherized blood of Christ Jesus has lived in the earth's ether ever since the Mystery of Golgotha. The earth's etheric body is permeated by what has become of the blood that flowed down on Golgotha. That is important. Had this not happened, humanity on earth would merely have continued as described before. As it is, it has become possible since the Mystery of Golgotha for the etheric blood of the Christ to take effect in the stream that rises up from below in us. Because the etheric blood of Jesus of Nazareth is present in the earth's etheric body, his etherized blood streams with the etherized human blood from below upward, from the heart to the brain. Therefore, not only what I described earlier happens in us, but also the human blood stream is united with that of Jesus Christ. These two blood streams can become one only if we learn to understand the Christ impulse in the right way. Otherwise no union will take place. Instead, the two streams, which were drawn together, will repel each other. We must acquire such understanding in a way that is suitable for each stage of Earth evolution. When Christ Jesus lived on earth, the event that was imminent could be comprehended only by those who had come to his forerunner, John, to be baptized with the words written down in the Gospel. They received baptism so that they would change their sin—that is, the karma of their previous lives that had come to completion—and so that they would realize that the most important impulse of Earth evolution was about to descend into a physical body. Human evolution progresses, however, and in our present age it is important that we understand that the knowledge contained in spiritual science must be received; and that we gradually become able to fire up the streams flowing from heart to brain so that anthroposophy can be understood. We will then be able comprehend the event that has its beginning in the twentieth century: the etheric Christ, as contrasted with his physical appearance in Palestine; for we have arrived at the time when the etheric Christ will intervene in earthly life, and become visible to a small number of people in a kind of natural clairvoyance.

158 October 4–14, 1911, GA 131.

159 Rudolf Steiner had called Rosicrucianism as such a "foundation" in 1907 ("...that Rosicrucianism is a foundation, which has in fact existed in the West since the fourteenth century." GA 55, p. 176).

160 GA 264, p. 427.

161 Ibid., p. 432.

162 Ibid., p. 427.

163 Ibid., p. 434.

164 GA 156, p. 77.

165 GA 264, p. 431.

166 Ibid., p. 429.

167 See Herbert Hillringhaus: *Das Ende unseres Jahrhunderts und der Aufgabe der Rosenkreuzer*. Freiburg 1969, p. 25f.

168 See GA 264, p. 435.

169 Hella Wiesberger: "Die Geschichte des Seelenkalenders und des Kalenders 1912/13" in: *Beiträge zu Rudolf Steiners Gesamtausgabe*. No. 37/38, 1972, p. 26.

170 GA 130, p. 234.

171 "When Rudolf Steiner was once asked about the most effective way to prepare the soul for the experience of the etheric Christ, he said by following the course of the year

in meditation. 'The mysteries of the seasons are nature's gift to those who through meditation strive to come close to the sphere of the Christ.'" (Paul Regenstreif: *Christian Rosenkreutz und seine Mission*, p. 33). See Sergei O. Prokofieff's fundamental study: *The Cycle of the Year as a Path of Initiation. An Esoteric Study of the Festivals*. Tr. S. Blaxland-de Lange. London: Rudolf Steiner Press 1995.

172 See Steiner's willingness to make the meditations of the *Soul Calendar* available to soldiers fighting at the front in early 1918, inserted in Waldorf-Astoria cigarette packs (see Hella Wiesberger: "Der Anthroposophische Seelenkalender und der Kalender 1912/13." *Beiträge zur Rudolf Steiner Gesamtausgabe*. No 37/38, 1972. Although Rudolf Steiner frequently pointed out to members of the Anthroposophical Society how difficult the meditations of the *Soul Calendar* really were, and how much esoteric research had gone into them ("long years of esoteric experience and research are contained in these fifty-two verses" GA 143, p. 164), he still made them available unconditionally to the "outside world" ("to give something that has grown from our way of thinking, so that people can use it to move a step further on the spiritual path." Ibid., p. 202). In doing so, Steiner practiced, in an exemplary way, the expansion of Rosicrucian spirituality in the twentieth century; that is, the dissemination of Rosicrucian wisdom and inner development that had been kept strictly secret for many centuries.

173 "The Rosicrucians are a community that since the fourteenth century has cultivated a truly spiritual Christianity within European spiritual life. The Rosicrucian society, which (next to all outer historical endeavors) sought to unveil the deepest truth of Christianity to its followers, also referred to its followers as 'Johannine Christians'" (GA 112, p. 11).

174 GA 84, p. 8f.

175 GA 36, p. 308.

176 See Sergei O. Prokofieff: *Die Erste Klasse der Michael-Schule und ihre christologischen Grundlagen*. Dornach 2009, p. 394f.

177 Cf. Sergei O. Prokofieff and Peter Selg: *Das Erste Goetheanum und seine christologischen Grundlagen.* Arlesheim 2010. In English see "The First Goetheanum and Its Christological Foundations" in *The Creative Power of Anthroposophical Christology.* Great Barrington, MA: SteinerBooks 2012.

178 See Peter Selg: *Die Gestalt Christi. Rudolf Steiner und die geistigen Intentionen des zentralen Goetheanum-Kunstwerkes.* Arlesheim 2009. Esp. p. 27ff. In English: *The Figure of Christ: Rudolf Steiner and the Spiritual Intention behind the Goetheanum's Central Work of Art.* Tr. Matthew Barton. Forest Row, U.K.: Rudolf Steiner Press 2009.

179 With regard to these early intentions to found a school for spiritual science, see Peter Selg: "Rudolf Steiner und der Bau des Ersten Goetheanum" in: Sergei O. Prokofieff and Peter Selg: *Das Erste Goetheanum und seine christologischen Grundlagen.* Arlesheim 2010, p. 11-51. In English see "The First Goetheanum and Its Christological Foundations" in *The Creative Power of Anthroposophical Christology.*

180 Quoted from Christoph-Andreas Lindenberg: *Rudolf Steiner. Eine Biographie. Vol. 1. 1861-1914.* Stuttgart 1997, p. 531.

181 GA 109, p. 159.

182 Ibid., p. 155f.

183 GA 26, p. 14.

184 GA 62, p. 34.

185 GA 233a, lecture of January 6, 1924. For the significance of that deed, and the possibility of human freedom and intellectuality or "pure thinking" (and its relevance for the reappearance of the Christ in the etheric), see Sergei O. Prokofieff's essential descriptions in "Das Opfer der Rosenkreuzer" in Sergei O. Prokofieff: *Die Erste Klasse der Michael-Schule und ihre christologischen Grundlagen.* p. 422-441.

186 In his Dornach lecture of January 13, 1924, Rudolf Steiner gave an in-depth description of the conflict between Rosicrucians and contemporary natural sciences; and of the transformation of natural-scientific knowledge effected by them (GA 233a).

187 GA 130, p. 314ff.

188   Ibid., p. 316.
189   GA 141, p. 101.
190   Ibid., p. 320.
191   See Note 88.
192   GA 130, p. 318.
193   See Peter Selg: *Unbornness: Human Pre-Existence and the Journey toward Birth*. Tr. Margot Saar. Great Barrington MA: SteinerBooks 2010.
194   GA 141, p. 97.
195   GA 130, p. 319.
196   GA 141, p. 99.
197   GA 130, p. 318.
198   GA 141, p. 100f.
199   Ibid., p. 94.
200   GA 130, p. 321.
201   GA 141, p. 103.
202   GA 140, p. 202.
203   In his thoughts on Christian Rosenkreutz, Paul Regenstreif called attention not only to the cosmic constellation of the year 1604, on which Kepler commented in his treatise "On the Fiery Triangle" (the conjunction of Jupiter and Saturn in the fire sign of Sagittarius—a constellation that recurs only every 800 years), he also pointed out that according to Rudolf Steiner, a new era of philosophical consciousness had begun with (or soon after) the year 1600. "Those of our dear friends who have read the new edition of my book *Riddles of Philosophy* will have found that I distinguished four eras of philosophical development. A first era, to which I gave the title 'The World Conception of the Greek Thinkers,' stretches from around the year 800 or 600 B.C. to the birth of Christ, that is, to the time when Christianity first arose. A second era stretches from the beginning of Christianity to about the year 800 or 900 A.D., that is, up to the times of John Scotus Eriugena. Then, the third era, a period to which I gave the title 'The World Conceptions of the Middle Ages,' lasted from the year 800 or 900 to the sixteenth century, and the fourth from the sixteenth century to the present. That is the era in which

we live now" (GA 161, p. 33). Regenstreif wrote: "In the year 1604 Christian Rosenkreutz performed an important deed for the further evolution of earthly humanity, by sending Buddha to the sphere of Mars. We get a sense of how the deeds of the great leaders of humanity are related to important star constellations if we consider that Rosicrucianism was founded in 1413, that is, at the beginning of the fifth post-Atlantean age, and that around the year 1604 a new era of human consciousness dawned" (*Christian Rosenkreutz und seine Mission*, p. 8).

204 GA 141, p. 131f.

205 GA 130, p. 322.

206 GA 72, p. 50.

207 For the magazine's intentions and Alexander von Bernus' relationship to Rudolf Steiner and anthroposophy, see Mirko Sladek's *Alexander von Bernus* (written in collaboration with Maria Schütze). Nuremberg 1981.

208 GA 147, p. 132. Later (in 1923), Ferdinand Maack (1861-1930) went on to found a Rosicrucian order in Hamburg, parallel to the new foundation of the General Anthroposophical Society through Rudolf Steiner, whom Maack saw, and fought, as his main opponent. Cf. Harald Lamprecht: *Neue Rosenkreuzer. Ein Handbuch*. Göttingen 2004, p. 187-191.

209 The Annual Meeting of the Theosophical Society in Adyar decided at the end of December 1912 "to cancel the charter of the German Section." According to the General Report for 1912, Annie Besant said in a prepared opening address on December 27, 1912: "The German General Secretary, educated by the Jesuits, has not been able to shake himself sufficiently clear of that fatal influence to allow liberty of opinion within his section.... The only thing left for me to do, as President, in face of this unprecedented outrage of opinion within the T. S., is to cancel the charter of the National Society in Germany."

210 For this process see Sergei O. Prokofieff: *Die Geburt der christlichen Esoterik im 20. Jahrhundert und die ihr widerstrebenden okkulten Mächte*. Dornach 1997. In English as *The East in the Light of the West*. Parts 1-3.

211 Quoted from Christoph-Andreas Lindenberg: *Rudolf Steiner.*
Eine Chronik. 1861-1925. Stuttgart 1988, p. 387. In English:
Rudolf Steiner: A Biography. Tr. John McAlice.
Great Barrington, MA: SteinerBooks 2012.

212 In July 1918, Rudolf Steiner published his fundamental essay on the "Previous Concealment and Present
Revelation of Suprasensory Knowledge" in von Bernus'
magazine, *Das Reich.* The essay was about the radical
change in dealing with occult knowledge in history, or
in the history of consciousness. It was another contribution to historical and spiritual Rosicrucianism and to the
tasks of the late nineteenth and early twentieth centuries,
and a meaningful addition to the previous treatises on the
Chymical Wedding. Steiner did not mention Rosicrucianism
explicitly in this study, but described the changes in the soul-
life that are a necessary precondition for the outer change.
He ended with the future-oriented words: "We live in an age
where suprasensory knowledge can no longer remain the
secret possession of a few; it has to become the common possession of all those for whom the meaning of life is a stir-
ring inner necessity in this age. This need is working actively
now in the innermost souls of people, and to a much greater
extent than many would think. It grows and becomes the
demand for the equal treatment of suprasensory knowledge
and the knowledge of nature" (GA 35, p. 408).

213 GA 181, p. 453.

214 GA 35, p. 385.

215 Ibid., p 389; emphasis added.

216 Johann Valentin Andreae, who published his writings anony-
mously, emphatically renounced them later. In his autobiography he admitted authorship of the *Chymical Wedding,* but
referred to it as a "farce, full of adventurous appearances,"
trying to play down its significance as much as possible.
"Astonishingly, it was appreciated by some and explained
with fine research. It is nonetheless an insignificant little
work which was meant to describe the useless efforts of the
curious." (Johann Valentin Andreae: Edited by Paul Antony.

Heidenheim 1970, p. 38.) In 1619, three years after the publication of the *Chymical Wedding*, and following the fervent
response it provoked, he wrote in the final chapter of his
work *Turris Babel*: "Now then, ye mortals! You need not
wait for any other fraternity. The comedy is over. The *Fama*
introduced them and has now taken them away again. The
Fama says yes; now it says no!" (Quoted from Gerhard
Wehr: *Die Bruderschaft der Rosenkreuzer*. Cologne 2007, p.
34.) An essential aspect of Andreae's vehement denial and
renunciation was the fear of being suspected of heresy, and of
persecution, which he was keen to avoid. ("He finds himself
continuously obliged to utter personal confessions of faith
and assurances of his orthodoxy." Gerhard Wehr: *Christian
Rosenkreutz. Urbild und Inspiration neuzeitlicher Esoterik*.
Freiburg 1980, p. 83.).

In 1643 Andreae (who, seven years later, at the climax of his
ecclesiastical career, was to advance to the position of prelate
and general superintendent at Bebenhausen) wrote to Count
August von Braunschweig: "I am more than certain that the
Rosicrucians never existed in reality, but only in folktales"
(Carlos Gilly: *Die Rosenkreuzer als europäisches Phänomen
im 17. Jahrhundert*. Ed. Bibliotheca Philosophica Hermetica.
Amsterdam 2002, p. 56). In 1619 he had still been emphatic in
stating: "While I part company with the fraternity, I will never
part company with the true Christian fraternity that exudes the
scent of roses under the cross" (Quoted from Hans Schick: *Das
ältere Rosenkreuzertum*. Berlin 1942, p. 121). Also in 1619,
after the beginning of the Thirty Years' War, Johann Valentin
Andreae published his work *Christianopolis*, a Christian social
utopia that was connected with the Rosicrucian social impulse.
See Wilhelm Schmidt-Biggemann's study: "Von Damcar nach
Christianopolis." Andreae's *Christianopolis* as a conception
for the realization of Rosicrucian ideas." In: *Rosenkreuz als
europäisches Phänomen im 17. Jahrhundert*. Ed. Bibliotheca
Philosophica Hermetica. Amsterdam 2002, p. 102-133. See
Andreae's relationship to John Amos Comenius, the last
bishop of the Bohemian Brotherhood, in: "'Er hat uns die

Fackel übergeben…' Die Bedeutung Johann Valentin Andreaes für Johann Amos Comenius" by Martin Brecht, in: *Das Erbe des Christian Rosenkreuz.* Ed. Bibliotheca Philosophica Hermetica. Amsterdam 1988, p. 28-47. Another reason for Andreae's (and his friends') renunciation of Rosicrucian writings, apart from his fear of being persecuted and outlawed, was that the resonance they provoked contained many signs of alienation and distortion. On November 22, 1619, the pamphleteer Frederick Frick, who had tracked Andreae down, wrote in a letter to a friend: "The first author of the *Fama* and *Confessio R.C.* is a grand man who wishes to remain concealed for the time being. He wanted to test people's opinions and has had sufficient experience of that now." (Carlos Gilly: *Die Rosenkreuzer als europäisches Phänomen im 17. Jahrhundert.* Ed. Bibliotheca Philosophica Hermetica, p. 55).

217   GA 181, p. 295. Rudolf Steiner pointed out on December 9, 1923, in Dornach, that the inspiration did not pass through the "secretary" Andreae in a pure form, but had rather been distorted: "But everything revealed there went through the heads of people, even though those people did not understand it. It went through their heads, and was diluted and distorted. Magnificent, powerful poetry was turned into the chatter and jabber that the verses of the *Chymical Wedding Christiani Rosenkreutz* occasionally are. They are nonetheless revelations of something magnificent: powerful macrocosmic images, powerful experiences between the human being and macrocosm that arise majestically. If we read the *Chymical Wedding* with today's insight, we learn to understand these images. They are vague because they are still colored by the minds they passed through. But behind them something magnificent appears" (GA 232, p. 144). For Johann Valentin Andreae's transcription of the Rosicrucian manifestos and the *Chymical Wedding* in Tübingen (among his circle of friends of that time, a "secret fraternity" around the prominent physician and alchemist Tobias Hess, and the lawyer Christoph Besold), see Joost R. Ritman's study: "Die Geburt der Rosenkreuzerbruderschaft in Tübingen," in: *Die*

Rosenkreuz als europäisches Phänomen im 17. Jahrhundert.
Ed. Bibliotheca Philosophica Hermetica, p. 57-74. Andreae's
authorship of all three Rosicrucian writings was still strongly
disputed in Rudolf Steiner's lifetime. Because of meticulous
research it is now considered scientifically established.

218 GA 235, p. 211.
219 Quoted from Gerhard Wehr: *Die Bruderschaft der Rosenkreuzer*, p. 28.
220 See GA 35, p. 332-390.
221 GA 183, p. 119.
222 GA 177, p. 35.
223 GA 55, p. 188.
224 On May 22, 1907 Rudolf Steiner spoke in Munich about a
form of "initiation" granted to Goethe during his illness in
Frankfurt (after finishing his studies in Leipzig). Speaking
about the consequences of that initiation, he said: "Goethe was
not conscious of this [initiation] at first; it appeared as a kind
of poetic stream in his soul, and the way in which that stream
worked its way down into his various works was remarkable."
In the same context he spoke about Goethe's *Tale of the Green
Snake and the Beautiful Lily*: "Then the initiation appeared
ever more strongly; and finally, Goethe, after growing more
and more conscious of it, was able to produce the remarkable lyric poem that we know as the *Tale of the Green Snake
and the Beautiful Lily*. It is one of the most profound works
of world literature. Those who are able to interpret it in the
right way will know much about Rosicrucian wisdom" (GA
99, p. 13). According to Andreas Neider, Goethe was aware of
the connection between his *Tale* and the *Chymical Wedding*.
Neider quotes from Goethe's letter to Charlotte von Stein of
June 28, 1786: "I have read Christian Rosenkreutz' *Wedding*.
It is a beautiful tale to be told at the right time, once it has had
a rebirth. In its old skin it is no longer bearable." (In: Rudolf
Steiner: *Anthroposophie und Rosenkreuzertum. Ausgewählte
Texte*. Ed. Andreas Neider, p. 129).
225 GA 93, p. 294.
226 GA 181, p. 295.

227 See Francis A. Yates: *The Rosicrucian Enlightenment*. London, New York 2002. Yates wrote about a "movement which was to be cut short when only just begun" (ibid., p. 96). Considering the actual origins of the Rosicrucian stream in the thirteenth/fourteenth centuries, this is not correct; but it accurately describes the extent of opposition and destructive intention provoked by the publication of the first writings. "For orthodox theologians ... the Rosicrucians were nothing but Schwenckfeldians, Weigelians, enthusiasts, Anabaptists, concealed Jesuits, libertines, atheists, or even vermin, intent on reforming, that is, deforming, everything. For the Jesuit François Garasse, the Rosicrucians were a dangerous religion opposing religion and the state" (Carlos Gilly: "Die Rosenkreuzer als europäisches Phänomen im 17. Jahrhundert." In: *Die Rosenkreuz als europäisches Phänomen im 17. Jahrhundert*. Ed. Bibliotheca Philosophica Hermetica, p. 21). Rudolf Steiner spoke about the fundamental difference between the Rosicrucian school and the Jesuit principles (particularly with regard to human freedom and will) after Neuchâtel, in Karlsruhe on October 5, 1911 (GA 131). On the following day he said, looking back: "We must own as the most eminent achievement of Rosicrucianism since esoteric spiritual life began in the thirteenth century that any initiation today must most deeply appreciate and recognize as an independent aspect of human inner life, what we refer to as the most sacred center of the human will, as we indicated yesterday. And because the human will is overwhelmed, oppressed by the esoteric methods described yesterday, and led into a particular direction, true esotericism must reject this direction most decidedly" (GA 131, p. 59). As Rudolf Steiner pointed out in Dornach in 1923, a few months after the Goetheanum had fallen victim to the flames, the destructive resistance to anthroposophy (as another movement that "was to be cut short when only just begun") started after the Karlsruhe lecture cycle. "One can say that from certain sides the opposition against anthroposophy started just after that cycle" (GA 224, p. 148).

228 See Peter Selg: *Vom Logos menschlicher Physis. Die Entfaltung einer anthroposophischen Humanphysiologie im Werk Rudolf Steiners*. Vol. I. Dornach 2006, p. 318ff.

229 At the end of May 1917, Count Otto Lerchenfeld, a Bavarian Reich Counselor, wrote in his diary: "… I spent three hours today with Dr. Steiner in Motzstrasse. I can see the solution for everything in front of me. I know that there is no other." (Quoted from Christoph-Andreas Lindenberg: *Rudolf Steiner. Eine Chronik*. 1861-1925, p. 384. In English: *Rudolf Steiner: A Biography*.).

230 See Albert Schmelzer: *Die Dreigliederungsbewegung 1919*. Stuttgart 1991, p. 52ff. At the end of September 1917, Rudolf Steiner pointed out that Andreae's writings were certainly addressed to those who held positions of power in the world, and that they contained suggestions for a new social order. "They were addressed to heads of state, to the statesmen of his time. They were an attempt to found a social order that would correspond to true reality, not to maya." (GA 177, p. 37; see also the title of the *Fama* printed in Cassel in 1914 by Wilhelm Wessel: "*Fama Fraternitatis* of the Laudable Order of the Rosy Cross to all scholars and heads of state in Europe"). For Rudolf Steiner's efforts to present his ideas on the threefold social order to leading politicians of the German Reich and Austria-Hungary (the "statesmen of his time"), see Lindenberg: *Rudolf Steiner. Eine Chronik. 1861-1925*, p. 622ff. In English: *Rudolf Steiner: A Biography*.

230a For the connection between the idea of threefoldness and Michael, see GA 194.

231 GA 176, p. 366.

232 GA 177, p. 37.

233 Paul Regenstreif: *Christian Rosenkreutz und seine Mission*, p. 8. For the pre-war context of Rudolf Steiner's lectures on the Fifth Gospel, see my studies: *Rudolf Steiner und die Vorträge über das Fünfte Evangelium*. Dornach 2010, p. 15ff. (In English: *Rudolf Steiner and the Fifth Gospel)* and *Die Kultur der Selbstlosigkeit. Rudolf Steiner, das Fünfte Evangelium und das Zeitalter der Extreme*. Dornach 2006, p. 13ff. In

English: *The Culture of Selflessness. Rudolf Steiner, the Fifth Gospel, and the Time of Extremes.* Great Barrington, MA: SteinerBooks 2012.

234 Ludwig Polzer-Hoditz: *Erinnerungen an Rudolf Steiner.* Dornach 1985, p. 92.

235 GA 266c, p. 351.

236 See Jan Bonek and Tomáš Bonek: *Karlstein.* Prague 2007.

237 GA 181, p. 358, emphasis added.

238 See Peter Selg: *Marie Steiner-von Sivers. Aufbau und Zukunft des Werkes von Rudolf Steiner.* Dornach 2006, p. 145ff.

239 GA 198, p. 80.

240 GA 202, p. 256.

241 GA 204, p. 108.

242 GA 260a, p. 275.

243 Rudolf Steiner to Ita Wegman. In: Ita Wegman: "Notizbuch Nr. 72, 1927." Ita Wegman Archives, Arlesheim. Published in: Ita Wegman: *Erinnerung an Rudolf Steiner.* Ed. by Peter Selg. Arlesheim 2009.

244 GA 259, p. 75.

245 Concerning this time rhythm, see Gundhild Kacer-Bock: *Die Mysteriendramen im Lebensgang Rudolf Steiners.* Stuttgart 2008.

246 See GA 259 and my study "Rudolf Steiner und das zweite Goetheanum" in: *Vom Umgang mit Rudolf Steiners Werk.* Dornach 2007, p. 21-64.

247 GA 260, p. 271.

248 Ibid., p. 94.

249 GA 260a, p. 115.

250 GA 270, I, p. 81.

251 GA 260a, p. 190.

252 GA 260, p. 274f.

253 Ibid., p. 276.

254 For the concept and implications of the Michael School, see in particular Sergei O. Prokofieff: *Die Erste Klasse der Michael-Schule und ihre christologischen Grundlagen.* Dornach 2009.

255 See Peter Selg: *Rudolf Steiner und die Freie Hochschule für Geisteswissenschaft.* Arlesheim 2008. In English: *Rudolf*

Steiner and the School for Spiritual Science. Great Barrington, MA: SteinerBooks 2012.

256 GA 260a, p. 371.

257 See GA 232.

258 See GA 260.

259 At the end of the Christmas Conference, Rudolf Steiner said to the conference members: "My dear friends, carry your warm hearts, into which you have laid the Foundation Stone for the Anthroposophical Society; carry these warm hearts *to strong and healing acts into the world.* And help will be bestowed on you, so that your heads will be enlightened by what you all are intent on achieving with single purpose. Let us make that decision today, and pursue it with all our might. And we shall see that if we prove worthy, a good star will guide our intentions. Follow that good star, my dear friends. We shall see where the gods will guide us through the light of that star" (GA 260a, p. 284; emphasis added).

260 GA 233a.

261 GA 316. For the course's spiritual content and connection to the Christmas Conference, see my study *"Die Medizin muss Ernst machen mit dem geistigen Leben." Rudolf Steiners Hochschulkurse für die "jungen Mediziner."* Dornach 2006.

262 GA 186, p. 122.

263 GA 233, p. 118.

264 GA 260.

265 See Sergei O. Prokofieff: *Menschen mögen es hören. Das Mysterium der Weihnachtstagung.* Stuttgart 2002, p. 116f. In English: *May Human Beings Hear It! The Mystery of the Christmas Conference.* Forest Row, U.K.: Temple Lodge 2004.

266 See Willem Zeylmans van Emmichoven: *Der Grundstein.* Stuttgart 1990, p. 41ff. In English: *The Foundation Stone.* Tr. John Davy. Forest Row, U.K.: Temple Lodge 2002.

267 GA 13, p. 416.

268 GA 270, II, p. 79.

269 See Peter Selg: *Das Ereignis der Jordantaufe. Epiphanias im Urchristentum und in der Anthroposophie Rudolf Steiners.* Stuttgart 2008.

270 GA 260, p. 65f.

271 Ita Wegman: "In Erinnerung an die Weihnachtstagung." In: *Nachrichtenblatt* (Newsletter of the weekly journal) *Das Goetheanum*, April 26, 1925. See also Ita Wegman: *Erinnerung an Rudolf Steiner*. Arlesheim 2009, p. 68.

272 See GA 270, I-III.

273 GA 260, p. 270.

274 GA 130, p. 235.

275 See Peter Selg: "*Ich bleibe bei Ihnen.*" *Rudolf Steiner und Ita Wegman. München, Pfingsten 1907 — Dornach, 1923-1925.* Stuttgart 2007, p. 39ff. In English: *I am for going ahead. Ita Wegman and the Medical Section.* Tr. Margot Saar. Great Barrington, MA: SteinerBooks 2012.

276 From a meditation given to Ita Wegman by Rudolf Steiner in the fall of 1923. See J. Emanuel Zeylmans von Emmichoven: *Die Erkraftung des Herzens. Eine Mysterienschulung der Gegenwart. Rudolf Steiners Zusammenarbeit mit Ita Wegman.* Arlesheim 2009, p. 148ff.

277 Ibid.

278 See Ita Wegman: *Erinnerung an Rudolf Steiner*, p. 42ff.

279 Ita Wegman's letter to Albert Steffen of August 21, 1925. Ita Wegman Archives, Arlesheim.

280 "Das Krankenlager, die letzten Tage und Stunden Dr. Steiners." In: *Nachrichtenblatt*, April 19, 1925. See also Ita Wegman: *Erinnerung an Rudolf Steiner*, p. 46.

281 "Notebook no. 74, 1935." Ita Wegman Archives, Arlesheim. Published in: Ita Wegman: *Erinnerung an Rudolf Steiner*, p. 47.

282 Personal information from Hella Wiesberger.

283 GA 264, p. 330.

284 GA 110.

285 Elisabeth Vreede: "Die Bodhisattvafrage in der Geschichte der Anthroposophischen Gesellschaft." In: *Die Bodhissatvafrage*. Ed. Thomas Meyer. Basel 1989, p. 41. In English: *The Bodhisattva Question. Krishnamurti, Rudolf Steiner, Valentin Tomberg, and the Mystery of the Twentieth-Century Master.* Forest Row, U.K.: Temple Lodge 2010.

286 GA 266a, p. 406.

287 GA 264, p. 247.
288 Elisabeth Vreede: "Die Bodhisattvafrage in der Geschichte der Anthroposophischen Gesellschaft." In: *Die Bodhissatvafrage.* In English: *The Bodhisattva Question.*
289 See Peter Selg: *Rudolf Steiner (1861-1925). Aspekte einer inneren Biographie.* Verlag des Ita Wegman Instituts, Arlesheim 2010.
290 Ibid.
291 GA 346, p. 164.
292 GA 266a, p. 219.
293 Ibid., p. 225.
294 For the inner nature of the "Nathan soul," see GAs 114, 148, 152. In his lectures about the preliminary stages of the Mystery of Golgotha (GA 152), Rudolf Steiner described how the Nathan soul was permeated by the Christ-being three times before the turning point of time. Each permeation was brought about by a situation of danger or emergency for humanity, which the Nathan soul took part in at a cosmic level. In his lectures on the Fifth Gospel, Steiner characterized the specific quality the Nathan soul unfolded in the Luke Jesus, his "genius of heart" and his "unlimited capacity for love," which led him to take part in the life around him to the highest degree "From his earliest childhood, it was characteristic of him to feel the suffering and joys of others as if they were his own suffering and joys; he was able to empathize most profoundly with other souls" (GA 148, p. 285). Yet he had initially great problems with finding his way into the material earthly world and civilization. "Up to his twelfth year, he showed no interest in any of the cultural contents that can be learned at school" (ibid.). If one studies Rudolf Steiner's inner nature, his biography, and his work more deeply, it is striking how the same qualities appear in his earthly life. All his therapeutic initiatives are built on those qualities. See Peter Selg: *Rudolf Steiner und eine Zukunftskultur der Selbstlosigkeit. Über das "Fünfte Evangelium." Rudolf Steiner og fremtidens Uselviskhetskultur. Om det "femte evangelium."* Lecture

given in Oslo on October 15, 2006. Bilingual private edition. Norway 2010, p. 117-151. For Rudolf Steiner's relationship to the Nathan soul, see Sergei O. Prokofieff's important study: "Die Menschheitsaufgabe der nathanischen Seele." In: *Gemeinschaftsbildung im Lichte Michaels.* Edited by Richard Steel. Dornach 2010, p. 25-57.

295 For Rudolf Steiner's social qualities see Peter Selg: *Rudolf Steiner. Zur Gestalt eines geistigen Lehrers.* Dornach 2010. In English: *Rudolf Steiner as a Spiritual Teacher. From Recollections of Those Who Knew Him.* Tr. Catherine E. Creeger. Great Barrington, MA: SteinerBooks 2010.

296 GA 14, p. 60.

297 Notebook no. 74, 1935.

298 Ita Wegman: "Das Krankenlager, die letzten Tage und Stunden Dr. Steiners." In: Ita Wegman: *Erinnerung and Rudolf Steiner*, p. 65.

299 Notebook no. 42, 1933. In: Ita Wegman: *Erinnerung and Rudolf Steiner*, p. 46.

300 "An die Mitglieder!" In: *Nachrichtenblatt*, September 20, 1935. Ita Wegman: *Erinnerung and Rudolf Steiner*, p. 20.

301 Notebook no. 25, Fall 1925. In: Ita Wegman: *Erinnerung and Rudolf Steiner*, p. 21.

302 See Sergei O. Prokofieff: *Menschen mögen es hören. Das Mysterium der Weihnachtstagung.* Stuttgart 2002, p. 46ff. In English: *May Human Beings Hear It! The Mystery of the Christmas Conference.*

303 GA 131, p. 158.

304 Rudolf Steiner's Christmas Conference lecture of December 29, 1923, movingly expresses his immense *gratitude* for the destiny that had allowed him to find the ancient, disappearing mystery stream "at the last cosmic moment" (GA 233, p. 111ff.). See also the words addressed by Rudolf Steiner to the youth group around Wilhem Rath on the following morning (December 30, 1923), in: Wilhelm Rath: *Rudolf Steiner und Thomas von Aquino.* Basel 1991, p. 24.

305 GA 233, p. 113.

306 "Michael will become the guardian of anthroposophy

because in anthroposophy he hopes to find those willing to serve him and because he intends to guard anthroposophy through that service until the great teacher will return." In: "Nachrichtenblatt der Wochenschrift," *Das Goethenaum,* May 17, 1925.

307 Notebook no. 72, 1927. In: Ita Wegman: *Erinnerung and Rudolf Steiner,* p.21.

308 Ita Wegman Archive, Arlesheim.

309 Ibid.

310 Goetheanum Archive.

311 Cf. GA 270, III.

312 Ita Wegman's letter to Albert Steffen of March 16, 1926. Ita Wegman Archive, Arlesheim.

313 Goetheanum Archive. Quoted from Johannes Kiersch: *Zur Entwicklung der Freien Hochschule für Geisteswissenschaft. Die Erste Klasse.* Dornach 2005, p. 51. In English: *A History of the School of Spiritual Science. The First Class.* Tr. A. Meuss. Forest Row 2006. .

314 Lecture draft, March 1935. Ita Wegman Archive. Facsimile in Peter Selg: *Geistiger Widerstand und Überwindung. Ita Wegman 1933-1935.* Dornach 2005, p. 176.

315 Protokoll [Record], p. 256. Goetheanum Archive.

316 See J. Emanuel Zeylmans van Emmichoven: *Die Erkraftung des Herzens. Eine Mysterienschule der Gegenwart. Rudolf Steiners Zusammenarbeit mit Ita Wegman.* Arlesheim 2009.

317 Ibid., p. 177.

318 Emanuel Zeylmans van Emmichoven (who died on July 9, 2008) had not been aware of Ita Wegman's statement of November 19, 1930 (that she possessed a written document about the ritual act that preceded the handing over of the rose cross and her admittance as joint leader of the Michael School). I only came across the statement myself after his death, during my own research into Elisabeth Vreede in the Goetheanum Archive (2009). Emanuel Zeylmans did not address the question of whether the description of the ritual preceding the handing over of the rose cross was among Ita Wegman's esoteric documents. He published the text as part

of his collection titled "The Great Rose Cross Mediation";
but remained uncertain about its content and its time of
origin. ("It is unfortunately not possible to date this important exercise. In the context of the other exercises I would
assume that it goes back to the fall of 1923." *Die Erkraftung
des Herzens. Eine Mysterienschule der Gegenwart. Rudolf
Steiners Zusammenarbeit mit Ita Wegman.* p. 177).

319 See the exercises in Rudolf Steiner's and Ita Wegman's hand-
writing from p. 105.

320 See Ita Wegman's numeration on p. 107 and Emanuel Zeylman
van Emmichoven's corresponding comments in *Die Erkraftung des Herzens,* p. 175.

321 English translation taken from: Rudolf Steiner, *Breathing the
Spirit. Meditations for Times of Day and Seasons of the Year.*
Forest Row 2007. Tr. M. Barton, p. 64.

322 Ibid.

323 Ibid., p. 333.

324 Ibid., p. 404ff.

325 Ibid., p. 139ff.

Notes to the FAMA FRATERNITATIS. From *A Christian Rosenkreutz
Anthology.* Compiled and edited by Paul M/ Allen

1   Theophrastus, Paracelsus of Hohenheim.

2   That is, the Reformation.

3   That is, Christmas Day.

4   *Rotae Mundi*—A kind of cosmic "clock" or "wheel," described
by Raimundus Lullus (1235-1315) in his *Ars Magna* and later
by G.W.V. Leibnitz (1646-1716) in his *De Arte Combinatoria.*
See also Rudolf Steiner, Lecture 10 in *The Apocalypse of St.
John.* Hudson, NY: Anthroposophic Press 1993.

5   "After 120 years I will open."

6   1484.

7   For *unius* read *vivus.* "This compendium of the Universe I
made in my lifetime to be my tomb."

8   "Jesus is my all."

9 "1. A vacuum exists nowhere.
2. The yoke of the Law
3. The Liberty of the Gospel
4. The Entire Glory of God."

10 "Theophrastus Paracelsus of Hohenheim."

11 or, "and which we daily communicate unfalsified."

12 Testament or Thesaurus.

13 "A Grain Buried in the Breast of Jesus. C. Ros. C., sprung from the noble and renowned German family of R.C.; a man admitted into the Mysteries and secrets of heaven and earth through the divine revelations, subtle cogitations and unwearied toil of his life. In his journeys through Arabia and Africa he collected a treasure surpassing that of Kings and Emperors; but finding it not suitable for his times, he kept it guarded for posterity to uncover, and appointed loyal and faithful heirs of his arts and also of his name. He constructed a microcosm corresponding in all motions to the Macrocosm, and finally drew up this compendium of things past, present, and to come. Then, having now passed the century of years, though oppressed by no disease, which he had neither felt in his own body nor allowed to attack others, but summoned by the Spirit of God, amid the last embraces of his bretheren he rendered up his illuminated soul to God his Creator. A beloved Father, an affectionate Brother, a faithful Teacher, a loyal Friend, he was hidden here by his disciples for 120 years."

14 By the choice of Fr. C. H., head of the Fraternity.

15 "Out of God we are born, in Jesus we die, through the Holy Spirit we are reborn."

16 The Fourth Kingdom. See Daniel 7: 16-28.

17 "Under the shadow of thy wings, Jehovah."

Bibliography

Works by Rudolf Steiner referred to in the text and notes, listed in English when available. All German titles are from the Rudolf Steiner Gesamtausgabe (GA), published by Rudolf Steiner Verlag, Dornach, Switzerland.

GA 13   *An Outline of Esoteric Science.* Tr. Catherine E. Creeger. Great Barrington, MA: SteinerBooks 1997. *Occult Science, An Outline.* Tr. G. and M. Adams. Rudolf Steiner Press, republished 2005. In German: *Die Geheimwissenschaft im Umriss.*

GA 14   *Four Mystery Dramas.* Tr. Ruth and Hans Pusch. Great Barrington, MA: SteinerBooks 2007. In German: *Vier Mysteriendramen.*

GA 15   *The Spiritual Guidance of the Individual and Humanity: Some Results of Spiritual-Scientific Research into Human History and Development.* Tr. Samuel Desch. Great Barrington, MA: SteinerBooks 1992. In German: *Die geistige Führung des Menschen und der Menschheit.*

GA 26   *Anthroposophical Leading Thoughts.* Tr. George and Mary Adams. Forest Row, England: Rudolf Steiner Press 1998. In German: *Anthroposophische Leitsätze.*

GA 28   *Autobiography: Chapters in the Course of My Life.* Tr. Rita Stebbing. Great Barrington, MA: SteinerBooks 2006. In German: *Mein Lebensgang.*

GA 34   *Lucifer–Gnosis* [Lucifer-Gnosis] (1903–1908): 2nd edition. 1987.

GA 35   *Philosophy and Anthroposophy.* Tr. Harold Jurgens. Spring Valley, NY: Mercury Press 1965. In German: *Philosophy und Anthroposophy.*

GA 36   *Der Goetheanumgedanke inmitten der Kulturkrisis der Gegenwart* [The Goetheanum-idea in the middle of the present cultural crisis] (1921-1925): 1st edition 1961.

GA 44   E*ntwurfe, Fragmente und Paralipomena zu den vier Mysteriendramen* [Sketches, fragments, and paralipomena on the four mystery dramas] (1910-1913): 2nd edition 1986.

GA 52   *Spirituelle Seelenlehre und Weltbetrachtung.* [Spiritual teachings on the soul and observations of the world]: 2nd edition 1986.

GA 55   *Supersensible Knowledge.* Tr. Rita Stebbing. Hudson, NY: Anthroposophic Press 1987. In German: *Die Erkenntnis des Übersinnlichen in unserer Zeit und deren Bedeutung für das heutige Leben.*

GA 57   *Wo und wie findet man den Geist?* [Where and how does humanity find the spirit] (1908/09). 2nd edition. 1984.

GA 62   *Spiritual Research: Methods and Results.* Tr. Paul M. Allen, Adam Bittleston, Elisabeth Tapp, Michael Tapp. Blauvelt, NY: Rudolf Steiner Publications 1981. In German: *Ergebnisse der Geistesforschung.*

GA 72   *Freiheit – Unsterblichkeit – Soziales Leben* [Freedom– immortality – social life] (1917/18): 1st edition. 1990.

GA 84   *Was wollte das Goetheanum und was soll die Anthroposophie?* [What was the intention of the Goetheanum and Anthroposophy?]: 2nd edition 1986.

GA 88   *Über die astrale Welt und das Devachan* [On the astral world and the devachan](1903–1904): 1st edition 1999.

GA 93   *The Temple Legend: Freemasonry and Related Occult Movements: From the Contents of the Esoteric School.* Forest Row, U.K.: Rudolf Steiner Press 2002. In German: *Die Tempellegende und die Goldene Legende als symbolischer Ausdruck vergangener und zukünftiger Entwickelungsgeheimnisse des Menschen.*

GA 98   *Natur- und Geistwesen – ihr Wirken in unserer sichtbaren Welt* [Nature beings and spirit beings: their effect on our visible world] (1907–1908): 2nd edition 1996.

GA 99   *Rosicrucian Wisdom.* Forest Row, U.K.: Rudolf Steiner Press 2002. In German: *Die Theosophie des Rosenkreuzers.*

GA 109   *The Principle of Spiritual Economy: In Connection with Questions of Reincarnation.* Tr. Peter Mollenhauer.

Hudson, NY: Anthroposophic Press/SteinerBooks 1986. In German: *Das Prinzip der spirituellen Ökonomie im Zusammenhang mit Wiederverkorperungsfragen.*

GA 110   *The Spiritual Hierarchies and the Physical World: Zodiac, Planets, and Cosmos.* Tr. René Querido. Great Barrington, MA: SteinerBooks 2008. In German: *Geistige Hiearchien und ihre Wiederspiegelung in der physischen Welt. Tierkreis, Planeten, Kosmos.*

GA 112   *The Gospel of St. John and Its Relation to the Other Gospels.* Tr. Samuel and Loni Lockwood, revised by Maria St. Goar. Great Barrington, MA: SteinerBooks/ Anthroposophic Press 1982. In German: *Das Johannes-Evangelium im verhältnis zu den drei andern Evangelien, besonders zu dem Lukas-Evangelium.*

GA 113   *The East in the Light of the West.* Blauvelt, N.Y.: Garber Communications 1986. In German: *Der Orient im Lichte des Okzidents.*

GA 114   *The Gospel of St. Luke.* See *According to Luke.* Tr. Catherine E. Creeger. Great Barrington, MA: SteinerBooks 2001. In German: *Das Lukas-Evangelium.*

GA 117   *Deeper Secrets of Human History in the Light of the Gospel of St. Matthew.* Tr. D.S. Osmond and A.P. Shepherd. Hudson, N.Y.: Anthroposophic Press/ SteinerBooks 1985. In German: *Die tieferen Geheimnisse des Menschheitswerdens im Lichte der Evangelien.*

GA 118   *Das Ereignis der Christus-Erscheinung in der ätherischen Welt.* (See *The Reappearance of Christ in the Etheric.* Great Barrington, MA: SteinerBooks 2003).

GA 126   *Occult History: Historical Personalities and Events in the Light of Spiritual Science.* London: Rudolf Steiner Press 1982. In German: *Okkulte Geschichte.*

GA 129   *Wonders of the World: Ordeals of the Soul, Revelations of the Spirit.* London: Rudolf Steiner Press 1983. In German: *Weltenwunder, Seelenprüfungen und Geistesoffenbarungen.*

GA 130   *Esoteric Christianity and the Mission of Christian Rosenkreutz.* London: Rudolf Steiner Press 1984. In

German: *Das esoterische Christentum und die geistige Führung der Menschheit.*

GA 133   *Earthly and Cosmic Man.* Blauvelt, NY: Garber Books 1986. In German: *Der irdische und der kosmische Mensch.*

GA 139   *The Gospel of St. Mark.* Tr. S.C. Easton. Hudson, NY: SteinerBooks/Anthroposophic Press 1986. In German: *Das Markus-Evangelium.*

GA 140   *Life between Death and Rebirth.* Tr. René M. Querido. Great Barrington, MA: Anthroposophic Press/Steiner-Books 1968. In German: *Okkulte Untersuchungen über das Leben zwischen Tod und neuer Geburt.*

GA 141   *Between Death and Rebirth.* Tr. E.H. Goddard and D.S. Osmond. London: Rudolf Steiner Press 1975. In German: *Das Leben zwischen dem Tode und der neuen Geburt im Verhältnis zu den kosmischen Tatsachen.*

GA 143   *Erfahrungen des Übersinnlichen* [Experiences of the suprasensory] (1912): 4th edition 1994.

GA 147   *Secrets of the Threshold.* Tr. Ruth Pusch. Great Barrington, MA: SteinerBooks 2007. In German: *Die Geheimnisse der Schwelle.*

GA 148   *The Fifth Gospel: From the Akashic Chronicle.* Tr. Anna Meuss. Forest Row, U.K.: Rudolf Steiner Press 1998. In German: *Aus der Akasha-Forschung. Das Fünfte Evangelium* (1913/14): 5th edition 1992.

GA 151   *Human and Cosmic Thought.* London: Rudolf Steiner Press 1991. In German: *Der menschliche und der kosmische Gedanke.*

GA 152   *Approaching the Mystery of Golgotha.* Tr. Michael Miller. Great Barrington, MA: SteinerBooks 2006. In German: *Vorstufen zum Mysterium von Golgatha.*

GA 156   *Inner Reading and Inner Hearing.* Tr. Michael Miller. Great Barrington, MA: SteinerBooks 2008. In German: *Okkultes Lesen und okkultes Hören.*

GA 161   *Wege der geistigen Erkenntnis und der Erneuerung künstlerischer Weltanschauung* [Paths of spiritual realization and renewal of the artistic worldview] (1915): 2nd edition 1999.

GA 176   *The Karma of Materialism.* Tr. Rita Stebbing. Spring
Valley, N.Y.: Anthroposophic Press 1985. Also: *Aspects of
Evolution.* SteinerBooks/Anthroposophic Press 1987.
In German: *Menschliche und menschheitliche Entwick-
lungswahrheiten. Das Karma des Materialismus.*

GA 177   *The Fall of the Spirits of Darkness.* Tr. Anna Meuss. Forest
Row, U.K.: Rudolf Steiner Press 2008. In German: *Die
spirituellen Hintergründe der äußeren Welt. Der Sturz
der Geister der Finsternis.*

GA 181   *Earthly Death and Cosmic Life.* Blauvelt, NY: Garber
Books 1989. In German: *Erdensterben und Weltenleben.
Anthroposopische Lebensgaben.*

GA 183   *Die Wissenschaft vom Werden des Menschen* [The
science of the development of the human being] (1918):
2nd edition 1990.

GA 186   *The Challenge of the Times.* Tr. Olin D. Wannamaker.
Hudson, NY: Anthroposophic Press 1961. In German:
*Die soziale Grundforderung unserer Zeit—In geän-
derter Zeitlage.*

GA 194   *Die Sendung Michaels.* (See *The Archangel Michael.* Tr.
Marjorie Spock. SteinerBooks/Anthroposophic Press 1994).

GA 198   *Heilfaktoren für den sozialen Organismus* [Aspects of
wellbeing for the social organism] (1920): 2nd edition
1984.

GA 202   *The Bridge between Universal Spirituality and the
Physical Constitutuion of Man.* Tr. D.S. Osmond.
Great Barrington, MA: SteinerBooks 2007. In German:
*Die Brücke zweischen der Weltgeistigkeit und dem
Physischen des Menschen* (1920).

GA 203   *Die Verantwortung des menschen für die weltentwick-
lung* [Human beings in connection with the cosmos]:
2nd edition 1989.

GA 204   *Materialism and the Task of Anthroposophy.* Hudson,
NY: Anthroposophic Press 1987. In German: *Perspektiven
der Menschheitsentwickelung.*

GA 224   *Die menschliche Seele in ihrem Zusammenhang mit
göttlich- geistigen Individualitaten.* [The human soul

and its connection with divine-spiritual individualities] (1923). 3rd edition 1992.

GA 232 *Mystery Knowledge and Mystery Centres.* London: Rudolf Steiner Press 1997. In German: *Mysteriengestaltungen.*

GA 233 *World History and the Mysteries in the Light of Anthroposophy.* Tr. George and Mary Adams; D. Osmond. London: Rudolf Steiner Press 1997. In German: *Die Weltgeschichte in anthroposophischer Beleuchtung und als Grundlage der Erkenntnis des Menschengeistes.*

GA 233a *Mysterienstätten des Mittelalters* [Mystery sites of the middle ages]: 5th edition 1991. Partly in English: *Rosicrucianism and Modern Initiation.* London: Rudolf Steiner Press 1982.

GA 235 *Karmic Relationships. Vol. I.* Tr. George Adams, rev. M Cotterell, C. Davy, D.S. Osmond. London: Rudolf Steiner Press 1988. In German: *Esoterische Betrachtungen karmischer Zusammenhänge. I.*

GA 240 *Karmic Relationships Vol. 6.* Tr. D. S. Osmond. London: Rudolf Steiner Press 1971. In German: *Esoterische Betrachtungen karmischer Zusammenhänge VI.*

GA 258 *The Anthroposophic Movement.* Tr. Christian von Arnim. London: Rudolf Steiner Press 1993. In German: *Die Geschichte und die Bedingungen der anthroposophischen Bewegung im Verhältnis zur Anthroposophischen Gesellschaft. Eine Angregung zur Selbstbesinnung.*

GA 259 *Das Schicksalsjahr 1923 in der Geschichte der Anthroposophischen Gesellschaft* [The year of destiny 1923]: (1923) 1st edition 1991.

GA 260 *The Christmas Conference for the Foundation of the General Anthroposophical Society 1923/1924.* Tr. Johanna Collis. Verses in text tr. Michael Wilson. Hudson, NY: Anthroposophical Press/SteinerBooks 1990. In German: *Die Weihnachtstagung zur Begründung der Allgemeinen Anthroposophischen Gesellschaft. 1923/24.*

GA 262 *Correspondence and Documents. 1901-1925.* Tr. Christian and Ingrid von Arnim. Hudson, NY: Anthroposophic Press 1988. In German: *Rudolf Steiner/Marie Steiner-von Sivers: Briefwechsel und Dokumente (1901-1925).*

GA 264 *From the History and Contents of the First Section of the Esoteric School 1904-1914.* Tr. John Wood. Great Barrington, MA: SteinerBooks 2010. In German: *Zur Geschichte und aus den Inhalten der ersten Abteilung der Esoterischen Schule 1904-1914.*

GA 265 *Freemasonry and Ritual Work. The Misraim Service: Texts and Documents from the Cognitive-Ritual Section of the Esoteric School 1904-1914.* Tr. John Wood. Great Barrington, MA: SteinerBooks 2007. In German: *Zur Geschichte und aus den Inhalten der erkenntniskultischen Abteilung der Esoterischen Schule von 1904-1914.*

GA 266/1 *Esoteric lessons (1904-1909) Volume I.* Tr. James H. Hindes. Great Barrington, MA: SteinerBooks 2007. In German: *Aus den Inhalten der esoterischen Stunde. Band I* (1904-1909).

GA 266/3 *Esoteric Lessons 1913-1923. Vol. 3* Great Barrington, MA: SteinerBooks 2011. In German: *Aus den Inhalten der esoterischen stunden. Band III.*

GA 268 *Mantrische Sprüche. Seelenübungen Band II* [Soul exercises. Vol. 2]: (1903-1925). 1st edition 1999.

GA 270 *Reimagining Academic Studies.* Tr. Judith Wermuth-Atkinson. Great Barrington, MA: SteinerBooks 2012. In German: *Esoterische Unterweisungen für die erste Klasse der Freien Hochschule für Geisteswissenschaft am Goetheanum 1924.*

GA 284 *Rosicrucianism Renewed. The Unity of Art, Science, and Religion. The Theosophical Congress of Whitsun 1907.* Tr. Marsha Post. Great Barrington, MA: SteinerBooks 2007. In German: *Bilder okkulter Siegel und Säulen.*

GA 316 *A Course for Young Doctors.* Spring Valley, NY: Mercury Press. In German: *Meditative Betrachtungen und Anleitungen zur Vertiefung der Heilkunst.*

GA 346 *The Book of Revelation and the Work of the Priest.* Tr. J. Collis. Forest Row, U.K.: Rudolf Steiner Press 2001. In German: *Vorträge und Kurse über christlich-religiöses Wirken, Bd. 5, Apokalypse und Priesterwirken.*

THE PATH OF THE SOUL AFTER DEATH: *The Community of the Living and the Dead as Witnessed by Rudolf Steiner in his Eulogies and Farewell Addresses* (2010)

RUDOLF STEINER'S INTENTIONS FOR THE ANTHROPOSOPHICAL SOCIETY: *The Executive Council, the School for Spiritual Science, and the Sections* (2011)

On Anthroposophical Medicine and Curative Education:

I AM FOR GOING AHEAD: *Ita Wegman's Work for the Social Ideals of Anthroposophy* (2012)

THE CHILD WITH SPECIAL NEEDS: *Letters and Essays on Curative Education* (Ed.) (2009).

ITA WEGMAN AND KARL KÖNIG: *Letters and Documents* (2009)

KARL KÖNIG: MY TASK: *Autobiography and Biographies* (Ed.) (2008)

KARL KÖNIG'S PATH TO ANTHROPOSOPHY (2008)

On Child Development and Waldorf Education:

I AM DIFFERENT FROM YOU: *How Children Experience Themselves and the World in the Middle of Childhood* (2011)

THE ESSENCE OF WALDORF EDUCATION (2010)

UNBORNNESS: *Human Pre-existence and the Journey toward Birth* (2010)

A GRAND METAMORPHOSIS: *Contributions to the Spiritual-Scientific Anthropology and Education of Adolescents* (2008)

THE THERAPEUTIC EYE: *How Rudolf Steiner Observed Children* (2008)

Ita Wegman Institute
for Basic Research into Anthroposophy

Pfeffinger Weg 1 A CH-4144 Arlesheim, Switzerland
www.wegmaninstitut.ch
e-mail: sekretariat@wegmaninstitut.ch

The Ita Wegman Institute for Basic Research into Anthroposophy is a non-profit research and teaching organization. It undertakes basic research into the lifework of Dr. Rudolf Steiner (1861–1925) and the application of Anthroposophy in specific areas of life, especially medicine, education, and curative education. The Institute also contains and cares for the literary estates of Ita Wegman, Madeleine van Deventer, Hilma Walter, Willem Zeylmans van Emmichoven, Karl Schubert, and others. Work carried out by the Institute is supported by a number of foundations and organizations and an international group of friends and supporters. The Director of the Institute is Prof. Dr. Peter Selg.

CPSIA information can be obtained at www.ICGtesting.com
Printed in the USA
BVOW071333290712

296440BV00001B/6/P